PLAYING

First published in the UK in 2012 by
Apple Press
7 Greenland Street
London NW1 0ND

www.apple-press.com

ISBN: 978 1 84543 455 7

Conceived, designed and produced by
Quid Publishing
Level 4, Sheridan House
114 Western Road
Hove BN3 1DD
England

Printed and bound in China

1 3 5 7 9 10 8 6 4 2

PLAYING

CARDS

The complete guide to:
- ♠ *52 Games* ♠
- ♦ *52 Tricks* ♦
- ♣ *52 Skills* ♣

Rob Beattie

APPLE

Contents

Tricks

Introduction

There's something about opening a new pack of cards. It doesn't matter whether you buy them at a filling station to while away a few hours on the road or if they're a classic deck of Bicycle cards bought specifically for a poker night—they smell the same. There's the same whiff of possibility, of hands to play or chances to take, of bets to win and of fun just waiting to be had.

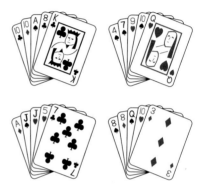

My dad carried a cribbage board with him all through his time in the army. I've been looking at it again recently. It's a bit battered—he got blown up in North Africa and carried some shrapnel in his forehead for the rest of his life—but it's still serviceable, and it cheers me to think of him and his mates settling down for a game of "crib"—a touch of normality and order amidst all that madness.

I remember how strongly a game of cards was built into our Christmas

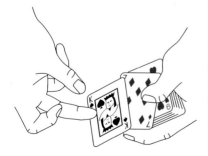

routine at home, first on the day at our house, and then the next day at Auntie Jean's. Her and Uncle Ern would take mum, dad, and me on at rummy, and as I got older there'd be a small sherry or the odd glass of beer to make me feel more grown up, part of an adult world where cards were the pastime of choice. Later, at university my friends and I would waste—well, waste is perhaps a little harsh—almost an entire summer playing a strange variation of Klabberjass; going through the attic the other week, I even found one of our old score sheets. We played literally hundreds of games, occupying hour after hour.

This book started as a small attempt to say thanks to the people who taught me the joy of cards, but along the way it became something else. Talking to

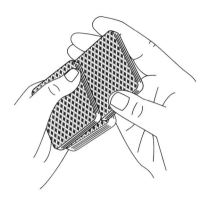

The Skills
Shuffles, cuts, ribbon spreads, fans, flourishes, false cuts, forces, false shuffles, finger lifts, double lifts… they're all here, explained in a simple step-by-step fashion that makes it easy for anyone to pick them up.

The Tricks
Here we've concentrated on tricks we think are easy and approachable because there are few things more frustrating than trying to do something that's simply out of your league or utterly beyond your physical abilities. Thus, you won't find any magician's glue or funny specialized decks of cards; there are few props, and no fiendishly complex sleights and palms… and there are definitely no cards up anyone's sleeves.

We hope the result is a book that you'll be able to come back to again and again, whether it's to brush up on your shuffling or because you fancy learning a new game or a new trick for the holidays. If you do that, then this book has served its purpose.

Oh, and always remember, it's not the cards in your hand that count, it's how you play them.

people who love cards and watching them play made me aware of how much skill is involved in the mechanics of a good shuffle or a nice cut, of how hard it is to do a decent ribbon spread or any of the moves that make a good game of cards such a pleasure to watch and be a part of. In turn that led me to other ways these techniques can be used, and thus, a whole section on card tricks was born.

So, we've ended up with a book in three parts that breaks down as follows:

The Games
There are thousands of games we could have included, but along with some of the most popular, we've also chosen those we think are the most fun, the most challenging, and the most exasperating. Also, much of the beauty of card games is that they vary so much, and we've included plenty of tips for trying something a bit different. Of course, when faced with so many variations and different games it would be impossible to include them all here; we only hope that you like the ones we have squeezed in.

Section 1

Games

Game

BeatYour Neighbour Out of Doors

Number of players: 2–4
Cards used: 52
Difficulty: 2
Also known as: Beggar Thy Neighbour, Battle

Objective

To win all the cards in the pack.

How To Play

This simple card-capture game is quick to learn and suitable for all ages; it's particularly good for encouraging kids and adults to play together because there's no actual skill involved and thus, adults don't have any advantage. The result? Kids will enjoy it more.

Divide the pack equally between the players, dealing the cards face down. Nominate someone to start and begin to play. Each person lays down a card face up – without looking at it first. This is important because BeatYour Neighbour relies on surprise for its wow factor.

Let's say there are two people playing. The first player lays down a card face up. If it's a plain card, from 2 to 10, then the second player lays down a single card on top of it. If it's a face card however, the second player must lay down penalty cards laid as follows: one card for a jack, two for a queen, three for a king

and four for an ace. If all the cards in the penalty sequence are suit cards from 2 to 10, then the first player wins the hand and takes all the cards, adding them to the bottom of their deck. Player one then lays down a new card to start the second hand. However, if the sequence of penalty cards laid by player two includes another face card, then the play switches and player one must lay down the appropriate sequence of penalty cards. This continues until one player lays penalty cards that contain no face cards, when the player who laid the last face card picks up the pile. The winner is the player who ends up with all the cards.

Variation: Battle

Battle is a dumbed-down – if that is really possible – version of Beat Your Neighbour Out of Doors. Split the pack between the players, dealing the cards face down. Player one turns over the first card, followed by player two. Whoever has the highest card wins the hand. If the cards are the same, that hand is set aside and taken by the winner of the next hand. It's that simple.

Tactics

There aren't really any, as it's all about chance. However, jacks are the most valuable cards, as the probability of winning the hand on the turn of a single card is greater than when trying to turn two, three or four.

On rare occasions, it's possible to get stuck, with two players just going round and round – if that's the case, each player should shuffle their hand and then carry on as before.

On the extremely rare occasions when this doesn't work and play continues, there are some known variations to solve the problem. First, you can agree to swap hands; second, each player cuts the other person's hand and whoever gets the highest card shuffles their hand while the loser does not; third, after both players shuffle they fan out their cards face down and do a blind swap of a pre-agreed number of cards – usually no more than six of them.

These are the penalty cards for Beat Your Neighbour Out Of Doors laid out in order: one for a jack, two for a queen, three for a king and four for an ace.

A typical hand of Beat Your Neighbour. Player one lays the king, player two starts to lay three cards, but on the third lays a queen. Play switches and player one lays two cards. The second of these is an ace, so player two must now lay four cards. Her fourth card is a jack, so player one must lay a single card. It's a suit card so player two wins the entire trick.

Game
Clock

Number of players: 1
Cards used: 52
Difficulty: 5
Also known as: Big Ben, Clock Patience

Objective
To reveal the entire pack.

How To Play
Lay down a clock face of cards, starting at 12 o'clock and then going clockwise through one, two, three and so on. That'll account for 12 cards. Lay a 13th in the centre. Next, go round each number on the clock, laying an additional card until each 'hour' of

Lay the cards out in a clock face, placing four cards on each 'hour' and three in the middle. The final card is the start card.

the clock has four cards and the centre has three. You should then be holding a single card in your hand, which is the one that you start with.

Look at the card in your hand, then place it face up under the pile of four cards with the same number; ace represents one, then the cards round the clock count as normal, finishing with 10, jack, queen and the king in the middle.

Once you've laid the card face up, pick up a card from the top of the same pile and then place that card face up on the bottom of the pile of the corresponding 'hour'. So, if your first card is a 9, pop it under the pile of 9s and pick up the top card; if that's a 7, pop it under the 7s and pick up that top

card; which is a 3, so put it under the 3s; and so on. The game ends when you turn over the fourth king and place it in the pile on the middle. You win the game when there are no cards left face down.

A finished game: The final card turned over is the fourth king. However, because there are still cards left unturned, this is a losing game. To win, all of the cards should be face up.

Game
Spades

Number of players: 4
Cards used: 52
Difficulty: 4

Objective

Players contract to win a specific number of tricks.

How To Play

Four players form two partnerships. Cut to see who deals and then each player gets 13 cards, face down; the pack is rated ace high and, unsurprisingly, spades are always trumps. After the first hand, the deal moves left each time.

Starting with the player to the dealer's left, everyone declares the number of tricks they're going to win – scoring is like Knockout Whist, so the highest card in the lead suit wins unless it's trumped with a spade, in which case the highest trump wins. Players do not have to outbid each other and may choose anything up to 13.

Overbidding

The nature of Spades encourages partners to overbid because they get rewarded rather than penalised for scoring more than they predicted. Spades gets round this by punishing consistent overbidders with a penalty. Make a note of each time partners bust their bids and when the total reaches 10, deduct 100 points from their score.

Alternatively, if they have a terrible conventional hand, they can bid 'nil' to win no tricks at all – then they only have to help their partner to win their bidded tricks.

The player to the dealer's left starts. They can lay what they like, except for a spade. Everyone must follow suit if they can. No one can lead with a spade until one has been laid by another player who couldn't follow suit, or who had nothing but spades in their hand. At the end, add up the number of tricks. The partnership that has won at least as many tricks as it predicted gets ten points for each one, plus an additional point for every trick over the bid.

Halfway through a hand – the player on the left has led with the king of diamonds and the next player the 8. The third player has no diamonds and may therefore lay a trump if they wish.

Game

Shed

Number of players: 2–6
Cards used: 52
Difficulty: 5
Also known as: Karma, Palace

Objective

Not to be the last person left holding
any cards.

How To Play

Each player gets three cards, dealt face
down in front of them, and then three
more, dealt face up on top of these. They
then get a further three cards to play as
a hand. From now until you play the six
cards in front of you, each player must
always have a minimum of three cards in
their hand.

First, everyone can swap one or more of
the cards in their hand with their face-
up cards – the idea being to have the
strongest three face-up cards possible.
Depending on the variation you play,
the strongest cards are 2s, 3s, 10s and
jokers; after that it's ace high. To decide
who starts, go from the dealer's left and
find the first player who has a 3 face up
in front of them. If no one has, it's the first
person with a 3 in their hand. If there are
no 3s out yet, it moves to 4s, then 5s and
so on until one is found.

The aim of the game is to get rid of your
cards by laying them face up next to the
deck either singly, in pairs or as three or
four of a kind. Player one starts and then
the next player must lay a card or cards
equal to, or higher than, the face-up card.
As each player lays down cards, they
must pick up from the remainder of the
deck to ensure they never hold fewer
than three cards. The pack is ranked ace
high, with 2s being high or low. If jokers
are included – you need them in a six-
person game – they are transparent and
switch the direction of play, so the player
who follows must match or beat the card
before the joker was laid. If a player lays
a 10 it 'burns' the pile and you turn it face
down and put it to one side – this pile
is now no longer used – and start a
new pile; laying or completing four of
a kind also burns the pile. Any player
who can't lay down a card from their
existing hand must pick up the entire
discarded pile. The following player
then starts a new one.

When all the cards in the deck have
gone, you play with the six cards in
front of you, starting with the three
face-up cards. If none of these allow you
to make a play, you must pick up the
discarded pile – now newly made from

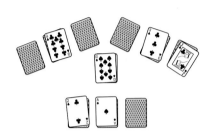

The start of a three-hand game. The dealer at the bottom has three strong face-up cards (2s can be high or low, ace is a high face card and the 10 will 'burn' the pile). The other hands don't look so good.

The endgame is in play. The dealer has just laid her 10 to burn the pack. After that she can lay either the 2 or the ace which are both strong cards.

your opponents' hands – and play with that until you get rid of all the cards in your hand, after which you can continue playing the cards in front of you. When you get down to the final three face-down cards you must play these without looking. The winner is the player who gets rid of their cards first. Players then drop out as they lay down their cards until one player is left, who is the loser.

Variations

There are plenty of variations of Shed, and most of these are made with regard to what the effects of each card are; for example:

- ♣ Laying an 8 switches play back the way it came.
- ♣ 10s can't be played on top of jacks, queens or kings.
- ♣ If someone lays a 7, then the next card must either be a lower card or another 7.

- ♣ If someone lays a 7, they can tell the next player whether they must go higher or lower.
- ♣ After a 9, the next player must lay a lower card.
- ♣ 3s are transparent, and the next player must follow the card that preceded the 3.
- ♣ Playing a 2 allows you to go again, playing any other card.
- ♣ Unless the first person to go out declares 'last card' at the end of their penultimate turn, they lose rather than win the game.
- ♣ Before the game, prepare a brown paper bag or a really terrible hat and make the loser wear it, or choose some other forfeit in advance.
- ♣ The list could go on, and you will rarely find two people who play the same variation of Shed. You can even alter the attributes of the cards yourself to add a little spice to your own games.

Game
Canasta

Number of players: 2–4
Cards used: 108 (two packs plus four jokers)
Difficulty: 8

Objective
The first to create enough melds and canastas and win 5000 points.

How To Play
This describes partner canasta, a four-player game. Partners sit opposite each other and everyone gets 11 cards, face down. Turn over the top card and place it face up next to the deck. If that card is a

joker, a 2 or the 3 of hearts or diamonds, turn it at right angles and then turn over another card and lay that across it. (This indicates that the pile is 'frozen' – see page 18.)

At each player's first go, they must lay any red 3s, face up on the table, away from play and replace them with cards from the pack. Then we're off. The order of each turn goes like this: pick up a card from the top of the deck, lay down one or more melds, or add to other melds, and lay down a card on the face-up pile.

A typical two-partner game showing various melds. The seven aces form a natural canasta, both partners have laid down their red 3s and both have used a wild card (a joker and a 2) to complete a meld.

Here are three examples of allowed melds: two 5s and a 2; two 7s and a pair of 2s; two queens and three 2s.

Here are three examples of disallowed melds: a 4 and a pair of 2s; two 6s and four 2s; three 2s.

Laying a black 3 across the pile like this 'freezes' it, restricting what other players can and can't pick up.

Each pair of partners tries to create melds that contain three or more of the same rank (excepting jokers and 2s, which are wild and 3s – see 'What's So Special About 3s?' on page 18); although partners can create separate melds, those that have the same rank must be combined into one. Melds can't contain more than three wild cards and must contain at least two 'natural' cards. Melds of seven or more form a canasta and you need at least one of these before you can go out; canastas also need at least four 'natural' cards. There are also special requirements for the first meld – see 'The First Meld' on page 18.

Play continues until one partner is ready to go out by either using all the cards in their hand to make a meld, or making a meld and discarding a final card. They can only do this if they've already laid a canasta and their partner agrees. Thus, you have to say 'Can I go out?' and if your partner says 'No' then you can't; if they say 'Yes' then you can.

Why might your partner say no? They may have cards in their hand that allow them to build up more melds and earn more points – remember that Canasta is a long-haul game and it's not always advisable to go out as soon as you can. The game is also finished when all the cards in the deck have been used.

At the end, you add up the points of the cards in your various melds as follows: jokers (50 points each), aces (20), 2s (20), 8s, 9s, 10s, jacks, queens, kings (ten), 4s, 5s, 6s, 7s and black 3s (five). Bonus scores also apply as follows: a natural canasta, which is a meld of seven or more cards that can't include wild cards (500); a mixed canasta, which is a meld of seven or more cards and can include wild cards (300); going out (100); a declared red 3 (100). If one partnership hasn't laid down any melds, take away 100 points for every red 3 they have (or 800 if they have all four).

Game
Canasta (continued)

There are other penalties too. If you're holding an undeclared red 3 you lose 500 points; try and go out without your partner's agreement and lose 100 points, take a face-up card illegally and lose 50 points.

The First Meld
You can't just lay any old meld to start, it has to meet the following requirement:

Score	Minimum Points
Less than 0	No minimum
0–1495	50
1500–2995	90
3000 or more	120

Freezing The Pile
Your opponents can 'freeze' the pile, limiting your options when it comes to picking up cards by laying any wild card at right angles on top. The pile is also frozen until you've laid down at least one meld or if the first card turned over is a red 3. How does this affect play? It means you can only take the pile if you've already got two natural cards in your hand and can use the top card to complete and lay down a meld. You can still take from the top of the deck, even if the pile is frozen.

Variation: Samba
- ♣ Needs three packs and six jokers, players get 15 cards.

What's So Special About 3s?
- ♣ *You can't use them to make melds, unless it's as part of the go on which you get out.*
- ♣ *Black 3s can be laid across the pile to freeze it.*
- ♣ *Red 3s can't be used in play at all but must be placed face up on the table.*
- ♣ *At the end of the game, each red 3 is worth 100 points; if a team has all four, they're worth a combined 800 points.*

- ♣ When it's your play, pick up two cards from the pack and discard only one.
- ♣ Lay down sequences (ace, 2, 3, 4 and so on) to score points, as well as melds.
- ♣ A seven-card set is a canasta, a seven-card sequence is a samba.
- ♣ No cards taken from the pack can be used to start a sequence.
- ♣ No sequences or sambas can include any wild cards.
- ♣ No melds can include more than two wild cards.
- ♣ A samba scores 1500, a natural canasta is worth 500 points, a mixed canasta scores 300 points, first partnership out scores 200 points and first to win 10,000 points wins.

Game
All Fours

Number of players: 2–4
Cards used: 52
Difficulty: 5
Also known as: Trinidad All Fours,
West Yorkshire All Fours, Lancashire All Fours

Objective
To score points by taking tricks.

How To Play
Best played by four people in pairs, sitting opposite each other. Deal the cards face up; when a player gets any jack, they become the 'pitcher' and the person to their right deals. After each hand, the deal – and pitch – goes left.

Everyone gets six cards. Aces are high and trumps are decided by the pitcher – whichever card she lays first is trumps. The pitcher's partner must not look at their hand until the first card has been played – so they can't tip their partner the wink about the choice of trumps. Once the first card is down, everyone has to follow suit or play a trump; if you can't do either, you can play any card. Highest trump or highest card of the leading suit wins the trick. When the first trick is won, it goes in front of the player who won it with one of the trump cards face up to remind everyone what's trumps. A player without trumps and no cards higher than 9 can lay all their cards face up on the current

trick and leave their partner to finish the game alone. Tricks are scored ace (four); king (three); queen (two); jack (one); and 10 (ten).

There are a maximum of four points to win in each game. The trick won by the highest trump gets a point, that won with the lowest trump wins a point, anyone who wins the jack of trumps in a trick gets a point, and the partnership that wins the most trick points overall gets a point.

Mid-game: The partners at top left and bottom right have won the first three tricks. The ace of clubs indicates trumps.

Game
Klondike

Number of players: 1
Cards used: 52
Difficulty: 7
Also known as: Solitaire

Objective
To build four piles of the four suits in order, starting with the ace.

How To Play
Make seven piles of cards in front of you from left to right as follows: a single card face up; a card face down with a card face up on top of it; two cards face down with a card face up on top; three cards face down and one face up on top; four cards face down with one face up on top; five cards face down with one face up on top; six cards face down with one face up on top; and seven cards face down with one face up on top. Put the remainder of the pack face down to form the pile.

You play the game by either working with the cards in front of you, or by turning new cards over from the pack, three at a time.

Look at the seven cards face up in front of you – the idea is to make piles of cards in number sequence, of alternating black and red suits, with the king at the base. Every time you reveal an ace – or one is turned over from the pack – it goes face up above the seven piles to form a foundation. There are four foundations, one for each suit. As each ace is revealed, you then try to build up the entire suit in sequence on top of it – ace, 2, 3, 4 and so on – so that you end up with four piles of cards: hearts, clubs, diamonds and spades.

You can move any number of cards between the seven piles, so long as they fit into the sequence – thus you can move a 6 of hearts, 5 of clubs and 4 of diamonds onto another pile where the current top card is the 7 of spades or clubs, but not if it's the 7 of hearts or diamonds because black and red suits must always alternate. Sometimes piles combine and disappear leaving a gap as the game unfolds, but you can start a new one if you have an available king – either as the bottom of an existing pile or by turning one over. You can't have more than seven piles at any one time though. When all the cards in the pack have been played, simply turn the pile over and – without shuffling them – start again until you've won the game or you can't go.

Variations

As if Klondike itself wasn't hard enough – some people put the chance of winning as low as one in 25 games – along comes Double Klondike. Played in exactly the same way, it adds a second pack, an additional two piles – making a total of nine – and four more 'get out' piles at the top, making a total of eight. Good luck with that!

Microsoft Solitaire

If you think you've seen or played Klondike before but can't remember where, you may be one of the billions of people who use Microsoft Windows on a personal computer. Klondike was shipped with Windows as Microsoft Solitaire and is probably the most popular – or at least most played – computer game of all time.

According to Microsoft, the highest possible score for Solitaire is 24,113. Using standard scoring and three-card draw, you'll get five points for every card that's taken from the deck and placed on one of the columns and then ten points for every card that goes to one of the four foundations at the top. Some genius programmer then decided that the game would award 700,000 points divided by the number of seconds it takes to finish the game. So now you know.

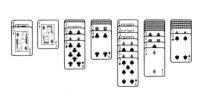

A hand of Klondike in progress. We've started to build up our piles of aces along the top, but we've also gone through the pack twice now and things aren't looking so good.

The slightly more formal layout of Microsoft Solitaire, the game included with millions upon millions of copies of Microsoft Windows – and actually a version of Klondike.

Game

Concentration

Number of players: 2+
Cards used: 52 or 104
Difficulty: 5
Also known as: Pelmanism, Memory

Objective
To pick up the most pairs.

How To Play
Deal out all the cards face down on the table in a 'cloud' so that they're scattered randomly, rather than dealt out in formal rows. The cards shouldn't touch just in case more than one gets turned over at a time by mistake. Each player takes it in turn to pick up two cards and look at them, without letting the other players see. If they're a matched pair – for example, two 7s, two 10s, a pair of jacks and so on – the player wins them and places them face down in front of him or her. Unmatched pairs are returned to their original position on the table. The key to winning the game is to remember where the unmatched cards are placed for when future turns produce the other half of the pair.

The game ends when all the cards have been picked up. The winner is the one with the most pairs. If you prefer a game with greater nuance, then play with only two people; this tends to produce a slow start, which accelerates toward a faster and flashier finish. Adding more players speeds up the overall game from the start. If you prefer a long, slow burn, then use two packs of cards.

Variations
For a generally faster game, deal the cards into rows. It'll also speed up play if each player reveals the cards they've picked up each time, rather than concealing them.

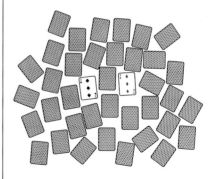

The start of a game of Concentration. Ordinarily, the first player to turn over a pair like this wouldn't reveal them to the other players, though some variations of the game allow this.

Game
Cribbage

Number of players: 2–3, or 4 in two partnerships
Cards used: 52
Difficulty: 8

Objective
To be the first past 120 points.

How To Play
We'll describe two-player Crib here to keep things simple. Cut the cards to see who deals – the dealer has an advantage. The dealer shuffles and deals six cards each. Both players look at their cards and discard two, face down; these four cards form the 'crib'. The first player lifts the top half of the pack and the dealer takes the top card of the remaining pile; the first player replaces the rest of the deck and the dealer turns the single card, face

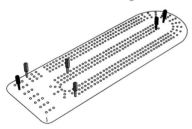

Cribbage comes with pegs and a board that you use to mark the score. Each player has two pegs – one to mark the current score and one to mark the previous score. The winner is the first one to 'peg out' by going over 120.

Scoring During The Play
Points
♣ When the cards add up to 15 you score two points.
♣ When the cards add up to 31 you score two points.
♣ If no one is able to make exactly 31, whoever is able to play the last card scores one point.

Pairs
♣ When you play a card that's the same as the previous one, score two points.
♣ When you play a card that's the same as the previous two, score six points.
♣ When you play a card that's the same as the previous three, score 12 points.

Runs
♣ When you complete a run of three or more, you score points equivalent to the number of cards in the run; runs do not have to be consecutive – for example, 3-2-4 will score three points for whoever lays the 4, and 5-6-7 will score three points for whoever lays the 7. Runs can be deceptive – for example, 7-5-4-8-6 doesn't become a run until the final 6 is laid, when the player wins five points. Remember that aces are low.

Game
Cribbage (continued)

up on top. This is the start card – if it's a jack, the dealer says 'two for his heels' and scores two points.

Player one lays his first card in front of him, face up and says the score out loud – aces score one, plain cards take their face value, face cards score ten. Player two lays a single card face down in front of her, adds the two cards together and says the total out loud. Player one lays a second card and says the total of the three cards and so on.

The hand continues until the total equals 31 or neither player can lay a card without busting 31. If a player is unable to go, they say 'go' and the other player continues for as long as they can. As you play the hand, score using the system in 'Scoring During the Play'.

When nobody can lay a card, the play ends and the show begins. Starting with the player who didn't deal, each person picks up the cards they laid down during the play, and looks for the scoring combinations outlined in 'Scoring During the Show'. After that, the dealer picks up the crib cards laid down at the beginning and counts combinations using the same system.

The Crib
So what goes into the crib, and what's it for? After a hand is played and the points have been taken from the play and the show, the crib cards are turned over and the dealer gets to use them in conjunction with the start card. Points are scored using the same system as for the show. So:

♣ *If you're the dealer, you need to lay two cards that you think may be useful later on, balancing that decision against the need to keep a strong hand with your remaining four cards.*
♣ *If you're not the dealer, then you want to discard your two least valuable cards because only the dealer gets to use the cards in the crib.*

Simple beginnings. The dealer scores two points because the turned card on the pack is a jack. Player one plays a 5, player two plays a king and scores two points for 15. Player one lays an 8 and player two follows with an 8 and scores two points for making 31 plus a further two points for completing a pair.

During the play this run is completed when the 7 of spades is laid down to make 5, 6, 7, 8 and scores four points.

Here's a nice scoring hand. Three 5s score six points, two kings score two points, three 5s add up to 15 and score two points, while various combinations of 5s and kings add up to 15 and score 12 points; this makes a total of 22 points.

During the show, a run like this scores six – three points for 2, 3, 4 and a further three for the same run using the second 3.

Scoring During The Show
The same card can be counted as many times as it forms part of a combination.

Points
Any combination that adds up to 15 scores two points.

Pairs
A pair scores two points; three of a kind scores six; four of a kind scores 12.

Runs
A run of three cards scores three points;

a run of four scores four; a run of five scores five. Note: Runs can be deceptive. A run of 2, 3, 3, 4 scores six – three points for 2, 3, 4 and another three made for the same run using the second three.

Flush
Four cards of a suit scores four. If the four cards are the same suit as the start card, score five.

One For His Nob
If you have a jack that's the same suit as the start card, score 'one for his nob'.

Game
Knockout Whist

Number of players: 2–7
Cards used: 52
Difficulty: 5
Also known as: Trumps

Objective
To win tricks and knock your opponents out of the game.

How To Play
A game of Knockout Whist consists of seven hands, starting with seven cards each. As each hand is played, the number of cards dealt to each player diminishes by one.

All the cards in a standard 52-card deck are used, with the cards of the four suits ranked in traditional order: ace, king, queen, jack, 10, 9, 8, 7, 6, 5, 4, 3 and 2. The dealer gives out seven cards to each player, clockwise, and then turns the top card of those that remain undealt face up to indicate which suit is trumps.

The game starts with the player on the left of the dealer, who leads with the first card. The next player must follow suit if they can – if not, they can play any card. Each trick is won by the highest trump card – if played – or the highest card of the suit laid down by the first player. At the next hand, six cards are dealt, then five at the next hand and so on until each player has only a single card left.

At the end of each hand, the player who wins the most tricks calls trumps for the next hand; if one or more players wins the same number of tricks then they cut the pack for trumps and the highest card calls. The advantage of winning a hand and choosing trumps becomes crucial as the number of cards in each hand decreases. Any player that wins no tricks in the course of a hand is knocked out.

To win Knockout Whist, the player must win the final hand, which is just one trick, where everyone has a single card each. Alternatively, if all the other players are knocked out before this hand is dealt, the surviving player wins the game.

Variation: A Dog's Life
A common variation on Knockout Whist is to introduce what's called 'a dog's life'. This applies to the first player who is unable to win a single trick in a hand.

Instead of being knocked out straight away, he or she gets a dog's life and at the next hand is dealt a single card, which he or she can play or pass – indicated by knocking on the table. If the person with the dog's life is immediately

to the left of the dealer, he or she may either lead that trick or knock and pass the lead onto the next player.

If two or more players are unable to win a single trick during the course of a hand – and assuming no one else has claimed the dog's life – they are all eligible to have one life each.

If a player who is on a dog's life wins a trick, then the player to their left leads the next trick – because the player on a dog's life only had one card. At the next hand, the player on the dog's life is dealt a normal hand with all the other players. If the player on a dog's life is unable to win a trick they are completely out of the game.

What Are Trumps?

How do you choose which suit should be trumps in a typical hand of Knockout Whist? Try these three hands and see how you get on:

♣ *In the first hand you are dealt: the ace of spades; 3, 7 and 9 of hearts; the queen of clubs; and the 2 and 10 of diamonds. Choose hearts because you have three of them – the ace and queen are high cards in their own right and may well win a trick without being trumps.*

♣ *In the third hand you are dealt: the 2, 3 and ace of diamonds; the king of clubs; and the jack of hearts. Choose diamonds because you have three of them, the other two cards are high and you may be able to draw out the other diamond face cards with your low 2 and 3.*

♣ *In the sixth hand you are dealt: the ace of hearts and the 7 of clubs. Choose hearts, because that will guarantee you win at least one of the two available tricks – nothing can beat the ace of trumps.*

Game

Piquet

Number of players: 2
Cards used: 32
Difficulty: 8

Objective

To form scoring combinations and win tricks.

How To Play

Remove all the 2s, 3s, 4s, 5s and 6s from the deck, leaving 32 cards that score ace high. Cut the cards to see who deals first and thereafter take it in turns. Tradition says that the deal must be either in twos or threes, but not both, and that

whichever you choose, both players must stick to it for the rest of the game. From this point on the dealer is called 'the younger' and the second player is called 'the elder'.

A game of Piquet is made up of six hands, called a partie. At the end of the partie whoever has the most points wins. In turn, each hand is made up of several stages:

The elder's hand in full. By exchanging two hearts he's reduced the strength of his hand in one way in the hope of getting some face cards.

The gamble has paid off to the extent that he now has four kings, which can't be beaten as a set because he also now holds three aces.

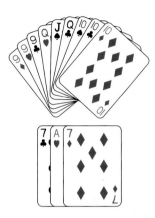

Because the elder took all five cards, there are only three left for the younger to exchange – he's picked three low cards to swap.

The replacement cards don't help much at all and this is going to be a tough hand to play.

♣ First, both players get 12 cards each and the remainder of the pack is placed in the middle face down.

♣ Second, both players, in turn, attempt to create scoring combinations by exchanging cards they don't want with the same number of cards from the remaining pack.

♣ Third, both players declare their combinations and the highest in each category scores points.

♣ Fourth, they play for tricks, scoring points for each one they win.

Having dealt the cards, both players examine their hands and look to see which of the point-scoring combinations they can make. At this stage if one player has no face cards in their hand, they can declare 'carte blanche' and score ten points straight away. They must then lay their cards quickly on the table, face up, one at a time to prove they've got no face cards before gathering them up into their hand again.

Assuming both players have face cards then they go about establishing which cards they think they should keep and which they should exchange for those left in the pack. Any discards are simply put to one side by each player and can be referred to later in the game if necessary. The elder goes first and must exchange between one and five cards; the discards are placed to one side face down and the replacements taken from the top of the remaining pack. If the elder takes only some of their allotted five cards they can quickly look at the other cards they were entitled to take but chose not to and then put them back. The younger goes next, exchanging between one card and however many are left. At the end of the exchange there may still be cards left in the pack, in which case

Game
Piquet (continued)

the younger can choose whether to flip them over so both players can see them or leave the remainder unturned – whichever they think offers the greater advantage.

The elder then checks their hand and tells their opponent which of the scoring combinations they can make in order: point, sequence and then set (see opposite). As they do, their opponent indicates whether or not they can challenge or beat that particular score in that particular combination. If they can, then they say 'not good', if they can't, then they say 'good' and if they have the same, then they say 'equal'. If they say 'equal' then the following happens:

Point scores – each player adds up the cards in their hand: ace scores 11, face cards score ten, and everything else has face value. Highest number gets to make the point score.

Sequence –the highest-ranking sequence of the same suit wins, so jack, queen, king beats 10, jack, queen.

Set – four of anything beats three of anything; elsewhere cards are ranked so there can be no tie.

If a point, sequence or set declaration passes unchallenged, the elder scores it, along with any other combinations of the same kind they hold in their hand; the younger scores nothing. The elder

The elder (top hand) hand looks stronger than the younger (bottom). However, the younger holds more cards of the same suit (four clubs) so can take the point score: four points (one for each card). The elder has the only sequence of three or more in the same suit (queen, king, ace) so takes the sequence score: three points (one for each card). Both players have sets (three or more cards the same) but the elder has four kings, which beats anything the younger has, so the elder scores for her four kings, three aces and three jacks: a total of ten points. Thus, before the trick taking starts, the elder scores 13 points, while the younger scores four.

At the end of the trick-taking phase, the elder has won nine tricks and younger has won three. Adding the points up, the elder has a total of 11 points, plus ten bonus points for taking more than seven tricks, plus another bonus point for taking the final trick; this makes a total of 22 points. The younger scores a total of five points. Add these to their respective scoring combinations and the elder has 35 points and the younger has just nine points.

then lays their first card and immediately gets a point for leading. At this point, any combinations called by the younger as 'no good' are counted and scored for him in the same way. It's important to understand that once the elder has declared a particular combination successfully, the younger cannot score any points for any cards he holds in that kind of combination – in other words, once a player has established they hold the highest sequence, they can score other lower sequences they may hold but their opponent cannot. If one of the players is able to score 30 or more before the trick-taking part of the game begins, they earn a bonus of 60 points, called *repique*. If the elder is able to score 30 or more by declarations or taking tricks, before the younger scores anything, they earn a 30-point bonus for pique. You cannot score pique if you've already scored repique.

Having declared your running scores, Piquet then becomes a trick-taking game where players earn a point for leading a

Combination Scores

When you examine your hand, here's what you're looking for and what each combination is worth:

♣ *Point: won by the person with the highest number of cards in a single suit; if you have six spades, for example, you'd say 'point of six' and if it was higher than your opponent you'd get six points. In other words, it's worth one point per card in the same suit.*

♣ *Sequence: three or more cards, running consecutively in the same suit; three cards score three, four score four, five score 15, six score 16, seven score 17 and eight score 18 points.*

♣ *Set: three or more cards of 10 or higher of the same type; three of a kind scores three points, four of a kind scores 14 points.*

Game
Piquet (continued)

trick and a point for winning a trick that was led by their opponent. There aren't any trumps, but you must follow suit and the highest card in the suit led wins the trick. At the end of the hand the person who takes the last trick wins an extra point. After that, there's a bonus of ten points for winning seven tricks (known as 'ten for the cards') followed by an additional 30-point bonus if you go on to win all 12 (called *capot*).

At the end of the final hand, the scores are totalled. Whoever has the highest score gets 100 points. If both players score over 100 points, find the difference between the two scores and add it to the winner's; should the loser not reach 100 points, his score is added to the winner's.

Tactics
Clearly, the heart of Piquet is the exchange and working out which cards to replace. Here are a few beginners' tips you'll find useful:

♣ If you're the elder, it may be tempting to only exchange four cards. Don't! You may like the idea of holding onto that extra ace, or whatever it is, but in fact it's always preferable to take all five cards, if only because it increases your chances of scoring one of the big bonuses: *repique* or *pique*.
♣ Always keep your longest suit intact.

♣ As well as thinking about your own cards, consider what your opponent is likely to have and try and keep a card or two in your hand that may stop them from completing any high-scoring combinations of their own.
♣ With the right cards it's possible to know if a combination will outscore your opponent. For example, if you have four jacks and a single queen, king and ace of different suits, you know that your four cannot be beaten.

Scoring Order
In order to establish if anyone's eligible to claim a repique or a pique it's important to remember that points are scored in order. The order runs like this:

Carte Blanche
Point
Sequence
Set
Trick Plays

Game
Matrimony

Number of players: 3+
Cards used: 52
Difficulty: 3
Also known as: Pope

Objective
To win the stakes in one of the five pots.

How To Play
Mark five squares on a piece of paper as below. At the start of every hand, players must place a set stake in each square – any unclaimed stakes are carried over to the next hand. The dealer shuffles the cards, deals one to each player face down, then another card to each face up. If any of the face-up cards is the ace of diamonds, that player takes the pot, the cards are gathered up and shuffled, new bets placed and a new hand dealt.

Each player in turn reveals their second card in the hope of making one of the pairs that will win the stake in one of the five pots. A king and queen wins the 'matrimony' pot, a queen and jack the 'intrigue' pot, a king and jack the 'confederacy' pot and a pair of anything wins the 'pair' pot; the 'best' pot is won by the player with the highest diamond in their hand. If two players have the same hand, you can cut the pack – highest card wins the pot.

Intrigue	**Matrimony**

Best

Confederacy	**Pair**

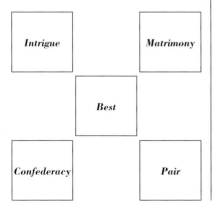

Part-way through a round with two hands revealed.

Game
Six Bid Solo

Number of players: 3
Cards used: 36
Difficulty: 5
Also known as: Frog, Crazy Solo

Objective
To win points by bidding and then winning tricks.

How To Play
Take out all the 2s, 3s, 4s and 5s, leaving a deck of 36 cards. The remaining pack is scored as follows: ace (11), 10 (ten), king (four), queen (three), jack (two) and everything else as zero. Cut to see who deals and then give each player 11 cards, leaving three that you lay face down to one side as a blind. Everyone checks their hand and the first stage of the game – the bidding – begins.

Everybody starts with 120 of whatever you choose to bet in, be they points, pennies, counters or matchsticks,

whatever you want to use; we'll call them pennies in this example. You'll also need a pen and paper to keep the score.

There are, as you may have guessed, six bids in Six Bid Solo going from low to high; the idea is that each player will try to outbid the others in order to play the hand solo.

The player to the dealer's left makes the first bid, or they can pass. Here are the bids and what they mean:

- ♣ Solo: chooses anything but hearts as trumps and will win 60 or more points
- ♣ Heart solo: chooses hearts as trumps and will win 60 or more points.
- ♣ Misère: no suit is trumps, and wins

The start of a hand of Six Bid Solo. We've turned the cards over to show the three 11-card hands. Player one (bottom left) passes, player two bids 'solo', hoping to get spades as trumps, while player three wins the bid with 'heart solo'. She'll now try to win 60 points or more with hearts as trumps.

The hand played out. Two players combined to score the top set of cards worth a total of 48, while the solo player at the bottom scored 56. The three cards in the middle are the blind pile and account for the other 16 points. In this case the solo player (bottom) loses and must pay each of his opponents the difference between his final score (56) and the 60 he bid, times three for each opponent. Thus, the loser pays out 12 pennies each to the others.

only tricks containing cards that don't score points (6, 7, 8 and 9).

♣ Guarantee solo: choose any suit as trumps and will win 74 or more points if it's hearts, or 80 or more points if any other suit is chosen.

♣ Spread misère: like ordinary misère except that after bidding has finished you must play the hand with your cards face up.

♣ Call solo: will win all 120 points. Before choosing the player may ask his or her opponents for any specific card to be swapped for a card of the caller's choice. If the requested card is in the blind, then there's no swap and he or she may call a different card.

If the first player bids and the next player bids a higher call (remember that the order of the calls explained above is from low to high), then these two players see who can make the highest bid. The moment that a player passes they cannot join in the bidding again. Once the first two players have bid in this way, the third player must bid against the previous high bidder or pass. Again, the first person of this pair to pass loses out of the bidding. The player who wins the bidding plays

solo against the others. If everyone passes, in other words if no one wants to make a bid, then the hand is scrapped, shuffled and dealt again.

Play begins to the dealer's left. Everyone must follow suit if they can, or trump if they can't; you can only discard if you can't follow suit and have no trumps left. Whoever lays the highest card wins the trick unless someone lays a trump in which case the highest trump wins. Remember that in both misère and spread misère there are no trumps.

If the single player called 'solo' and they win, they take two pennies from each opponent for every point they score over 60; if they lose, they pay each opponent two pennies for every point under 60. If a single player calls and wins 'heart solo' they win three pennies from each opponent for every point over 60; if they lose, they pay each opponent three pennies for every point under. All the other bids score the winner a specific number of points – a misère is 30, a guarantee solo is 40, a spread misère is 60 and a call solo is 100; a call solo in hearts wins 150; if they bid any of these

Game
Six Bid Solo (continued)

and lose, they forfeit the same number of points. In the unlikely event that the solo player scores 60 and the opposing pair score the same, nobody scores any points.

Variation: Frog

This is a simpler version of Six Bid Solo that's widely enjoyed in the southern United States and all across Mexico. The main difference between Frog and Six Bid Solo is that there are only three bids you can make instead of six. They go like this:

♣ Frog: must swap three cards for the blind before calling hearts as trumps.
♣ Chico: chooses any suit except hearts as trumps; the blind stays where it is.

♣ Grand: same as chico but hearts must be called as trumps.

For each bid, you have to take enough tricks to score 60 or more points, including those cards in the blind/discard. Call 'frog' and win any points above 60 from each player, win 'chico' and collect double, win 'grand' and collect triple. Call any of these and lose and you forfeit either single, double or triple the difference to each of your opponents.

This scoring system makes Frog an intriguingly high-scoring game to play – it's especially fun at the end of the evening, perhaps after a more sedate and complex game like Piquet.

The beginning of a hand of Frog. The player at the bottom left will bid 'frog', offering to exchange three cards for those in the blind before calling hearts as trumps. The top player will call 'chico', and the third player will pass – he can't outbid the others by calling 'grand' because he only has one heart.

Game
Klabberjass

Number of players: 2
Cards used: 32
Difficulty: 7
Also known as: Clubby, Klob, Clobyosh

Objective
To win points by winning tricks and making melds.

How To Play
Start off by removing the 2, 3, 4, 5 and 6 of each suit from the pack, so it leaves you with 32 cards (see box 'How They Score', on page 39, because it's unusual). Cut to see who deals – lowest card wins – and after that alternate the deal. Each player gets six cards. The next card is turned over and offered as trumps.

The non-dealer checks their hand and then says either 'take it' to accept trumps or 'pass' to reject it. If they accept trumps, the game continues; if they pass, the dealer can accept or reject trumps in the same way. If both players reject trumps then the hand is scrapped, the deal swaps and they try again. When trumps are accepted by either player, the trump card is placed face up, crossways under the deck. Each player then receives three more cards. Finally, the bottom card from the remaining pack is turned over and placed on top; this card isn't used but with such a small deck, knowing what it is can help either player – for example,

if it's a high-scoring card. Whoever chooses trumps is known as the 'maker'.

Each player then checks their cards. If either has the 7 of trumps, they can swap this for the turned trump card sitting crossways under the deck. Then the first stage of play begins. Each player tries to

The first six cards have been dealt to each player and the trump card has been turned and placed under the pack. The top player has passed on trumps but the dealer will accept them.

Game
Klabberjass (continued)

create melds or sequences of cards in suit, and in the following order: ace, king, queen, jack, 10, 9, 8 and 7. A four-card sequence scores 50 points and a three-card sequence scores 20. If two players have a three- or four-card sequence, the highest one wins – so king, queen, jack beats jack, 10, 9; if the sequences are exactly the same, they cancel each other out unless one is a trump sequence, in which case, that wins.

Having arranged their cards in sequence, the non-dealer lays their first card – we'll come to trick taking in a second. As they do, they must declare their melds by saying '20' for a three-card sequence or '50' for a four-card one. If unable to match the meld, their opponent then replies with 'good'. If able to beat it, he replies 'not good'. He can also ask for clarification; for example, 'how high?' or 'how many cards?' or 'in trumps?' Once the first trick has been played, whoever has the highest run must show it to their opponent so you can note the score for later. If they've got more than one meld, they show and declare them both.

Then the trick taking starts. The non-dealer goes first and you have to follow suit or trump – you can't just lay any old card if you have a trump that can beat what's in front of you. Highest card in a

particular suit or highest trump wins and the winner lays the first card of the next trick. If you've got the king and queen of trumps, you can score an extra 20 points by saying 'bella' when you play the second of the two cards. Whoever wins the final trick gets a bonus ten points.

When the hand is finished, count the number of points using the chart in the 'How They Score' box, adding any bonus points and meld scores. If the maker (whoever called trumps) wins

With trumps accepted the extra three cards have been dealt to each player. The top player calls '20' because he holds the queen, jack, 10, while the dealer must accept by saying 'good' because he has no melds.

more points, both players take the points they've scored and add them to their total. If the maker scores fewer points, then his opponent takes both scores; if the scores are equal, the maker earns nothing while his opponent takes his own score. The first player to score 500 points wins the game.

Variations

♣ When choosing trumps, a player may also say 'schmeiss', which means they'll either accept the trump or discard their hand – but that their opponent gets to choose which.

♣ If both players have exactly the same sequence, instead of cancelling each other out the non-dealer scores.

How They Score

During trick play the cards score high to low like this: for trumps, jack, 9, ace, 10, king, queen, 8, 7; for non-trumps, ace, 10, king, queen, jack, 9, 8, 7.

Card	Trump Score	Non-Trump Score
jack	20	2
9	14	0
ace	11	11
10	10	10
king	4	4
queen	3	3
8	0	0
7	0	0

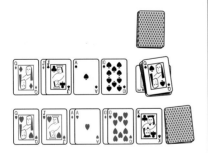

The hand played out. The top player scores three (a queen), four (two jacks), 11 (an ace) and ten (for the 10) plus ten points for winning the last trick and 20 points for the opening meld of three cards. That's a total of 58. The bottom player scores three (a queen), 20 (the jack of trumps), 22 (two aces), 20 (two 10s) and four (for the king), making a total of 69. Since the bottom player called trumps, both players receive their scores.

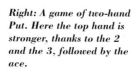
Game

Truc

*Number of players: **2** or **4***
*Cards used: **32***
*Difficulty: **5***
*Also known as: **Truco, Put***

Objective
To gain 12 points by winning hands.

How To Play
First, remove all the 2s, 3s, 4s, 5s and 6s from the deck, leaving 32 cards. Truc ranks cards in this order: 7, 8, ace, king, queen, jack, 10 and then 9. There are no trumps, you don't have to follow suit, and the highest card wins the trick.

Cut to see who deals. In a two-player game, you both get three cards. Check them. If the person who didn't deal doesn't like their hand they can request a new deal. If the dealer agrees, the hands are trashed and new cards are dealt, otherwise, you have to play on – and the dealer knows you don't much like your hand! The non-dealer lays a card and the dealer just has to

beat it – remember, there are no trumps and no need to follow suit; if both players lay the same card, no one wins the trick and the same player leads the next card.

Here's where the fun starts. You need 12 points to win a game, and each hand is initially worth one point. However, you can increase its overall value during play, upping it first

Left: A game of two-hand Truc with the cards turned over. The bottom hand is the strongest here, thanks to the 7 and 8 of diamonds, which score higher than anything else.

Right: A game of two-hand Put. Here the top hand is stronger, thanks to the 2 and the 3, followed by the ace.

In Partner Truc, the second partner can indicate to the boss whether they hold specific cards – a smile for a 7, a wink for an 8 and a shrug for an ace.

from one to two points and thereafter to four, then six, then eight, ten and 12. If the other player doesn't accept the increase, they must discard their hand and the first player wins whatever points were on the table before the increased bid was rejected.

Stakes can be raised once by each player during the course of a trick (thus the dealer could raise the initial single-point trick to two points and then lay a card; the second player can then raise from two to four before laying their own card). It's also possible to raise the stakes by bidding 'my remainder', which makes up the value of the bet to the full 12 points required to win the game. Your opponent can respond by trashing their hand (in which case they lose the number of points bid before the proposed raise) or by matching you

(in which case whoever wins the hand wins the game).

When the three tricks have been played, the winner of the game point (or points if the bid has been increased) is the one with two tricks; if one or more hands were 'tied' by laying the same card, then the winner of the first trick gets the game point(s).

Variation: Partner Truc
♣ Four players, in pairs, sit opposite each other.
♣ Each partnership has a 'boss'; and only the boss can increase the stakes and only the other boss can accept or reject it.
♣ Only the boss can request a new deal.
♣ The boss can tell their partner what cards to play – even though they don't know which specific cards are being held.

♣ The second partner can indicate whether they're holding specific cards by making signals such as a wink for an 8 or a shrug for an ace, when the other players aren't looking, of course!

Variation: Put
♣ A game for two players: each game is worth five points.
♣ Play with the full pack and score it thus: 3, 2, ace, king, queen and so on down to 4.
♣ Cut to see who deals.
♣ Trick winner lays next card first; after a tied hand, the player who put the first card down leads again.
♣ Either player can say 'Put' before they lay their card. If the other player accepts then the winner of the hand wins the game there and then; if they reject it, they discard their cards and the 'putter' wins a point.

Game
Old Maid

Number of players: 2+
Cards used: 52 (or 104 if more than six play)
Difficulty: 3
Also known as: Old Boy and Black Peter

Objective

To avoid being left with a queen of any suit: the old maid.

How To Play

If you're playing with six players or fewer, use a single deck of cards; if playing with more than six, use two decks. In either case, the dealer removes the queen of spades and then shuffles the pack before dealing all the cards out. It doesn't matter if one or more players have a different number of cards.

Each player goes through their hand, removing any matching pairs of cards – thus two jacks or two 7s or two 4s – and placing them face down on the table so the other players can't see what they are.

Then, the dealer fans out her hand – again face down – and offers the fan to the player on her left, who takes a card. If the new card allows that player to make a pair, she can add it to her pile of pairs on the table. If not, the second player simply retains the card. In either case the second player then offers her hand, face down and fanned out to the next player, who takes a card and tries to make a pair. The game continues like this until each player is able to lose all of her cards.

Having taken one queen out means that the unlucky loser is the one who's left holding the odd queen: the old maid. Beginners often make the mistake of playing Old Maid too thoughtfully, while fans of the game (and there are plenty) understand that playing it at speed makes it more entertaining.

Did You Know?

Old Maid began life as a simple drinking game – whoever lost would buy a round of drinks for the other players – and it's still popular with those who enjoy a liquid forfeit. In Victorian times, this element of the game was downplayed; instead, special packs of cards became more common that featured easily identifiable characters who could be matched up to form pairs. In decks such as these the last card was literally depicted as an old maid.

A typical hand of Old Maid, after the cards have been dealt and each player has begun removing any pairs they hold. Note the queen of spades at the top, which has been removed from the pack before dealing and the one remaining queen in the hand on the left.

Almost at the end of the game. Notice that the player on the left has managed to shift his queen to the player on the right. With only one or at most two turns left, the player on the right is running out of chances to pass the queen on.

Tactics

Lots of players kid themselves they can encourage others in the game to take a particular card by the way they position it in the fanned hand or by the way they offer it. The most consistent tactic, however, is to ignore the cards and watch the face of the player taking the blind card carefully – particularly toward the end of the game. Most people will give away the fact that they've taken one of the remaining queens. If they don't it's probably best not to play them at poker.

At the beginning of the game, it's tempting to organize your hand sequentially, starting with the low cards and moving up to the face cards. Don't! If you do, then when the time comes to start swapping cards, it won't take too long for your opponents to work out which end of the fanned hand they should take from to avoid the queen. Alternatively, you can bluff them by making it look as though you're arranging the cards in order while actually placing the queen where they might expect to find another, lower card in the hand.

Game
Pontoon

Number of players: 2+
Cards used: 52 (or 104 if more than eight players)
Difficulty: 5
Also known as: Blackjack, Twenty One, Vingt Un

Objective

To have a hand higher than the banker's, that doesn't score more than 21.

How To Play

Decide what you're going to use for betting – pennies, matchsticks, pistachio nuts for kids or proper money for adults – and then decide on the minimum and maximum stakes. Cut the pack to choose the banker. She then shuffles the pack and deals out two cards to everyone, face down. Everyone looks at their cards. If the banker has pontoon, she declares it there and then and wins the hand, job done.

If not, each player sets about acquiring a winning hand. Here's how the potential turns break down. If the first player has pontoon (an ace and a face card or 10) they lay their cards with the ace facing up and the other card facing down and call it. Play then moves on to the next player.

If the first player has two cards the same, he can split his hand by turning the cards face up. The dealer then lays a new card on each hand, face down – and these are then played and betted against as individual hands. Alternatively, you can 'buy' another card by increasing your bet – and keep buying cards for as long as your hand is less than or equal to 21. Don't want to bet any more? Then ask the banker for a 'twist', which gets you another card without having to bet. Once you've reached 15 (or more) you can 'stick' and play moves round to the next person. If buying or twisting increases the value of your hand over 21, then you are 'bust' and the banker takes your stake. The maximum number of cards you can have in your hand is five; after

> ### Did You Know?
> *To increase the popularity of the original Twenty One, casinos paid out many times more for any two-card 21 that included the jack of spades or the jack of clubs. This proved so successful that it led to the adoption of a new name for the game and it became Blackjack.*

that your turn is finished. Switching from 'buy' to 'twist' is a one-way street – once you've chosen to 'twist', you cannot 'buy' on the next turn. Each player completes their turn before the next person gets a go.

When all the players have finished, the banker turns her two cards face up and begins to deal extra cards for herself. If the dealer goes over 21 she busts and loses – paying out equivalent to the stakes of the other players. If she sticks on 21 or less with less than five cards, she collects from any players who have a lower value than her and pays those with a higher value. If she makes a five-card trick – the cards add up to 21 or less – she only pays players with pontoon.

High-scoring pontoon hands. Starting from the top and moving anticlockwise: a five-card trick (making 21), a four-card trick and a three-card trick (also both making 21); all three of these are beaten by pontoon (the king and ace), which in turn is beaten by banker's pontoon (the queen and the ace) as laid down by the banker.

If a player wins the hand with pontoon, they become banker and get to deal. If there are no pontoons, you add the cards to the bottom of the pack and the banker deals again.

Variations

As with most games, particularly those that are essentially betting games, there are many variations. Here are just a few:

- ♣ Instead of being able to stick on 15, choose a higher number.
- ♣ If you've got four cards that make 11 or less, then you're guaranteed a five-card trick and can only twist to get one rather than buying.
- ♣ Any player apart from the dealer who has three 7s has a 'royal pontoon' and cannot be beaten.
- ♣ An ace with a picture card beats an ace with a ten.
- ♣ You can only split your cards if you have two aces; other cards can't be split.

Game
Pig

Number of players: 2+
Cards used: 52
Difficulty: 4
Also known as: Spoons, Donkey

Objective

To be the first player to make four of a kind.

How To Play

Having decided how many people are going to play, the dealer removes the same number of sets of four from the pack. Thus, if three are playing, she might take out four aces, four 7s and four jacks and play with those; if six people play, she could take out a further four 9s, four 2s and four 8s. The dealer then puts the rest of the pack to one side and shuffles the cards thoroughly.

Each player then gets four cards that they must organize into four of a kind. When everyone's checked their hand, each person takes a card and lays it face down in front of the player to their left, who then picks it up and sees if it can be used to build toward or even complete a four of a kind.

Here's where the fun really starts. There's no concept of 'turns' or 'hands' in Pig. Instead, each player can pass and receive cards as quickly as they can – always making sure that they never

hold more than four cards in their hand at once. As soon as you have four of a kind, you rest your index finger against your nose in a manner that suggests you know something the others don't (you do – you've won the game). As soon as other players realize you've made the signal they must do the same, regardless

A hand of Pig at the beginning. Note that the number of players dictates the number of four of a kinds that are taken from the pack and dealt out. In this case, four players share 16 cards which are made up by four 4s, four 9s, four jacks and four queens.

of whether they have a hand with four of a kind. The last person to realize what's going on is the 'pig' or the 'donkey' in the most common variation, and loses the game.

If you want to extend the game, then give everyone a set number of lives; Pig players get three, while Donkey players get six. If kids are playing the game they can find the whole finger-by-the-side-of-the-nose movement too hard to pull off discreetly; sometimes this is entertaining and adds to the fun, but if it doesn't then they can choose a more subtle gesture like a wink or a gentle tap on the table. You can play Pig with up to 13 people or even more if you decide to add a second deck. It's definitely the kind of game that gets better the more people play.

Spoons is a variation of Pig in which the first player to make four of a kind must pick up a spoon from the middle of the table, followed by everyone else, until one player – the loser – doesn't have a spoon. Obviously, there should always be one less spoon than there are players.

Tactics

Speed during play is important, as is a smooth take-and-pass-on movement when receiving and giving cards. But the key is the sneakiness with which the winner can touch their nose; I've even seen, for example, someone with a four of a kind to 'accidentally' drop a card, bend to retrieve it, and come up with the finger placed subtly against their nose.

Variation: Spoons

Play the game exactly as outlined above, but with the addition of kitchen utensils! Place spoons in the middle of the table. Make sure there are one fewer than the number of players – and make sure everyone can reach them, or, if you're feeling somewhat cruel, then place them slightly too far away…. When the first player makes four of a kind, they grab a spoon. Everyone else goes for a spoon as well immediately. The loser is the person left without a spoon.

Spoons can be replaced with anything you like, and the weirder the objects the better the game. You have been warned!

Game
Nap

Number of players: 3+
Cards used: 52
Difficulty: 5
Also known as: Napoleon, Euchre

Objective
To win tricks from the other players.

How To Play
Shuffle the pack and then deal five cards to each player – usually as three to each, followed by a two to each. Each player examines their hand and then bids, depending on how many tricks they think they can win – three, four or 'Nap' (all five). After someone has called 'Nap', a subsequent player can call 'Wellington' for all five tricks, but wins, or loses, more points. Tricks are won using trumps (which the winning bidder picks) or by laying the highest card. Players must follow suit if they can.

The person who bids highest lays their first card, which becomes trumps for the hand. Each player follows suit if they can or discards a card they don't want. The highest trump wins the trick or – if no trumps are played – the highest card wins. Assuming the highest bidder wins the hand, he receives three, four, five and ten points for three, four, Nap and Wellington respectively. If he loses, he must pay each of his opponents however many points he would have won.

A pair of typical Nap hands. The player on the left would probably bid two tricks while the player on the right would bid three – and probably win!

Variation: Botheration
The rules are the same as for Nap, but with the following exceptions:
- ♣ Nominate a non-playing score-keeper.
- ♣ Deal the whole pack.
- ♣ Play with four or five people for the most fun.
- ♣ Aces are high.
- ♣ Having been dealt their hand, each player declares how many tricks they intend to win – anyone winning more or less scores nothing; anyone winning the correct number scores their hand plus ten points.

Game
Speculation

Number of players: 3–7
Cards used: 52
Difficulty: 4

Objective

To hold the highest trump at the end of the hand and win the pot.

How To Play

Establish a pot in the middle. The dealer has the advantage and so stakes more than the others – usually the dealer bets six while the remaining players bet four. Shuffle the pack and then deal three cards to each player, one at a time, face down. The dealer then turns the top card of the pack to reveal trumps; if it's an ace, the dealer wins the hand straight away – that's the advantage of being the dealer. Otherwise, the hand begins.

The player to the dealer's left reveals one of their cards. If it's a trump, they can keep it or sell it to the highest bidder. After that, players take it in turns to reveal a card, and keep or sell it (if it's a trump), until all of the cards are revealed – apart from the player who currently holds the highest trump, who misses a go until the hand ends or that trump is bettered by another player. Whoever has the highest trump at the end wins the pot. If no trumps are revealed, the pot is increased by the same as the initial bet.

Tactics

There are many ways to win Speculation. Clever selling of a not-so-high trump can actually get you more than is in the pot during the course of a game. In addition, remembering the high trumps gives you a better chance of predicting what cards the other players might be holding as the game goes on.

A three-hand game. The 9 of spades has been turned as trumps and the player to the dealer's left has started with a 7 of spades. No other trumps have been turned – and because the 7 is the highest trump, player one doesn't need to turn any more of his cards to win.

Game
Bezique

Number of players: 2
Cards used: two packs of 32 made by removing the
2,3,4,5 and 6 from each deck; this is known as a Piquet deck
Difficulty: 7
Also known as: Cinq Cents

Objective
To be the first player to reach 1000 points.

How To Play
Remove the 2s, 3s, 4s, 5s and 6s from two standard decks to create a 64-card Piquet deck. Then shuffle the remaining cards.

Each player gets eight cards – usually dealt as three, then two and then three. The dealer then takes the top card off the rest of the pack and places it underneath, but sticking out so both players can see it. This suit is then trumps – and if it's a 7 the dealer immediately scores ten points – welcome to the weird and wonderful world of Bezique! The game is divided into two parts – the play, which is a bit like Knockout Whist (see pages 26–7), and the declaration, which is more like Cribbage (see pages 23–5).

The player to the dealer's left begins by laying down a card. The dealer then replies with his own card. You don't have to follow suit until the whole deck is used up, then you must follow suit for

the remaining eight tricks if you can; this allows you to hang on to trumps if you think they'll be useful. Scoring the play is simple: any card higher than the original card in the same suit wins the trick. When you've won a trick, turn the cards face down and put them to one side.

The start of a game of two-handed Bezique. The eight cards have been dealt to each player and the dealer has turned the top card over and put it to the bottom of the pack as trumps. Because it's a 7, the dealer scores ten points immediately.

Scoring During Play

♣ 10s beat any other card except aces.

♣ Two queens of spades and two jacks of diamonds is a double bezique and scores 500 points.

♣ A 10, jack, queen, king, ace of the trump suit is a royal sequence and scores 250 points.

♣ A 10, jack, queen, king, ace of the same suit is a sequence and scores 100 points.

♣ Four aces scores 100 points.

♣ Four kings scores 80 points.

♣ Four queens scores 60 points.

♣ Four jacks scores 40 points.

♣ A queen of spades and a jack of diamonds is a bezique and scores 40 points.

♣ Two kings and two queens of trumps is a double royal marriage and scores 40 points.

♣ A king and queen of trumps is a royal marriage and is worth 40 points.

♣ Two kings and two queens of the same suit is a double common marriage and worth 20 points.

♣ A king and queen of the same suit is a common marriage and worth 20 points.

♣ A 7 of trumps scores ten points and can be exchanged for the trump card.

A selection of scores in Bezique. From left to right, starting at the top: 10 beats any other card in tricks except aces; a queen of spades and a jack of diamonds is a bezique; a 10, jack, queen, king and ace is a sequence and scores 100 points; four kings scores 80 points; a queen and a king of the same suit score 20 points; and a 7 of trumps can be exchanged for the turned-over trump card.

When the final card has been drawn from the pack, whoever wins the last trick scores an additional ten points. After that, you both play a final eight hands of tricks using the cards in your hand and any cards already laid down as melds. Note that for these final eight hands, you have to follow suit and must trump if you can't; only when you can't follow suit or trump can you lay another card.

When all the tricks have been played, count up the score from all the melds and then add ten points for each ace or 10 won in tricks.

The deal then changes hands and play continues until one of you reaches the magic 1000 points.

Then, see if you can lay down any of the combinations shown in the scoring table. Then record your points. After that, the trick winner takes a new card from the deck, followed by his opponent and the next hand begins.

Once a player has laid down a combination, he can use any of the cards as part of a trick or to form new, scoring combinations.

Game
Bezique (continued)

Variation: Chinese Bezique

Churchill's favourite includes these significant variations from ordinary Bezique:

♣ The deck is made up of six stripped decks as opposed to two.

♣ Deal each player 12 cards, three at a time – note: there is only one deal.

♣ If at the end of the deal the losing player has scored less than 1000 points, a 'Rubicon' occurs and the winning player scores 3000 points.

♣ You only choose trumps after one person has declared a sequence or a marriage.

♣ You can reuse cards to form another combination; for example, you make four queens and then draw a fifth that allows you to make a different four queens.

♣ Score 250 if you win the last trick.

♣ If you only hold 7s, 8s and 9s, you can declare 'carte blanche' and score 250 points – and keep scoring 250 points every time you draw another 7, 8 or 9.

♣ Because you've got so many more cards, the following 'extra' scores are possible: triple bezique (1500 points) and quadruple bezique (4500 points).

♣ In trumps, the following scores apply: four jacks (400), four queens (600), four kings (800), four 10s (900) and four aces (1000).

♣ When declaring bezique, it depends on what's trumps. If it's spades, then bezique is the queen of spades and the jack of diamonds; if it's hearts, then bezique is the queen of hearts and the jack of clubs; if it's clubs, it's the queen of clubs and the jack of hearts, and if it's diamonds, bezique is the queen of diamonds and the jack of spades.

♣ 10s and aces don't count and aren't included in the scoring.

In this six-pack variation of Bezique it's possible to call 'carte blanche' if you have a hand with no court cards like the one shown here.

Variation: Pinochle

The differences are as follows:

♣ Play with both decks but remove the 7s and 8s from the pack as well to make a 48-card deck.

♣ Each player gets 12 cards.

♣ Score by making combinations, not winning tricks.

♣ Each new combination must include a card that hasn't been used before.

♣ Combination types: dix (9 of trumps, worth ten points); pinochle (jack of diamonds and a queen of spades, worth 40); marriage (a king and queen, worth 20); double marriage (king and queen of trumps, worth 40); forty jacks (four jacks, one of each suit, worth 40); sixty queens (four queens, one of each, suit worth 60); eighty kings (four kings, one of each suit, worth 80); hundred aces (four aces, one of each suit, worth 100); flush (jack, queen, king, 10 and ace of trumps, worth 150).

♣ When no more combinations can be played, everyone then gathers up their hands and plays tricks, and each winning trick is worth one point.

Scores in Pinochle, from top left to bottom right, starting with ten points for the 9 of trumps and ending with 150 points for a flush: jack, queen, king, 10 and ace of trumps.

A Little History

As the setup of the deck suggests, Bezique is based on Piquet, another melding and trick-taking game that was popular in seventeenth-century France.

Although it's said that the writer Wilkie Collins (who wrote The Moonstone*) and the poet Christina Rossetti were fans of the game, its most famous exponent was Winston Churchill, Britain's wartime prime minister. Churchill was said to enjoy the more complex variation, Six-Pack or Chinese Bezique, and would play the game to relax at the end of the long and stressful days in office.*

Game
Cheat

Number of players: 2–10
Cards used: 52 or 104
Difficulty: 4
Also known as: I Doubt It

Objective
To get rid of all the cards in your hand.

How To Play
Start by dealing all the cards out, face
down to each player – it doesn't matter
if everyone doesn't get exactly the same
number. The player to the dealer's left
begins by laying – face down – between
one and four cards on the table and
saying 'aces'. The next player then does
the same thing, but lays down between
one and four 2s, saying '2s' as she does,
then it goes to 3s, 4s, 5s and so on until
you reach the kings. Then it goes back to
the ace again and you start over.

The point of the game is to get rid of all
your cards, but the twist is that you can
cheat to try and achieve this faster, and
you must try to hide your deceit from the
other players. Thus, the first player may
have no aces at all and instead lays down
two 3s and a 7 – and merely says 'aces';
the next player may have no 2s and
instead lays down a queen and a jack,
the third player may only have one 3, but
decides to lay that down with a 4 and a
jack and merely say 'threes', and so on.
If you suspect that one of your opponents

*Here's a hand of Cheat shown face up – it
would, of course, be played face down
so that players can cheat. Player one
has been honest and laid down two aces.
Player two sneaks in a dodgy 9 with her
pair of 2s, while the next person adds a 7
to the pair of 3s. Player one stays on the
straight and narrow with three 4s, while
player two takes her chances with a single
5 and two bogus cards: the 9 and 10.*

is trying to pull a fast one, then you
can call them out by saying 'cheat',
or whatever the name of the variation
you're playing is. If you catch them out,
then they have to pick up the entire
pack; if you're wrong, then you have to.
The winner is the one who's able to lay
down their final cards without being
successfully challenged.

'Cheat!' Player one has just claimed to have laid down 'three 6s'. However, since we're holding two 6s in our own hand, we know better and can shout: 'Cheat!'

If you decide to play with more than six people, add a second pack to make the game last longer.

Variations

There are plenty of Cheat variations – but don't worry, all of them involve copious amounts of cheating!

- ♣ Some games start with the ace and then go king, queen, jack, working their way down through the pack.
- ♣ Gamesters with time on their hands can try the single-card version, in which each player lays down their cards one at a time.
- ♣ There's also a variation in which you must lay down three cards each time, unless it's your final hand and you have fewer than three cards.
- ♣ You can elect to play cards above or below the previous card.

Tactics

Don't put the cards in your hand into order because it makes it easier for other players to work out what you're up to.

Try to remember your own cards – if you've genuinely laid down two 7s and have a third in your hand and someone else claims to be laying down two 7s, you know they're cheating. Similarly, if you've got good card-counting skills, pick two or three cards to follow carefully in case you can catch someone out; remember, of course, that any player may try and cheat at any time, so guesswork based on counting is just that – guesswork.

Game
Tien Len

*Number of players: **4***
*Cards used: **52***
*Difficulty: **6***
*Also known as: **Killer***

Objective
To win tricks and get rid of all your cards.

How To Play
Cut to see who deals, then shuffle well and deal 13 cards out to each player, face down. On the first hand, whoever has the 3 of spades – the lowest-value card in the pack – must lay it face up in the middle. The hand then goes clockwise round the four players. Each player has to lay a higher card than the preceding one. You don't have to follow suit, though you need to remember that some suits are worth more than others (see 'How to Score'), and you must lay the same number of cards as the person before you.

These are the plays you can make:

♣ Any single card – the first card of every hand must be the 3 of spades.
♣ Any pair – they don't have to be the same suit.
♣ Any triple – they don't have to be the same suit either.

A typical game begins: You always lay the 3 of spades first as this is the lowest card in the pack. Remember that 2s are high, so this card is currently winning the hand.

♣ Any 4 – they don't have to be the same suit either.
♣ A run of three or more consecutive cards, irrespective of suit – because 2s are high they can only be used after a king to make queen, king, ace, 2, for

This hand has started with a pair of queens followed by two aces. Player three couldn't go and it looks like player four can't either because the hand doesn't contain a pair of 2s, the only cards that can be laid on a pair of aces.

example, and not after an ace to make ace, 2, 3, 4.

♣ A double run of consecutive cards; for example, two 5s, two 6s and two 7s.

♣ You must follow the preceding card or cards – laying a single card to a single card, a pair to a pair and so on. You can't beat a three-card run with a four-card run, for example; you can only beat it with a higher

three-card run or the same run in a higher suit – for example, 8, 9, 10 of spades beats 4, 5, 6 of spades; and 4, 5, 6 of hearts also beats 4, 5, 6 of spades because of the suit order (see 'How to Score').

♣ Even if pairs or runs seem to be equal, there will always be a higher hand because of the difference in suit; just compare the highest card in the pair or run to find which uses the highest suit.

Of course, it wouldn't be a good game if there weren't exceptions to these rules, so here goes: a run of four can beat any single 2, but not any single card; a double run of three can also beat a single 2, but no other single cards; a double run of four can beat a pair of 2s, but no other pairs, and a double run of five pairs can beat three 2s but no other three of a kind. Phew!

As the game proceeds, everybody lays down cards to follow the player before them; if you can't go, you pass to the next player and do not lay again until the current

hand is finished. A hand is finished when no other player can legitimately lay another card or cards. Then, the person who laid the last card or cards puts the face-up pile to one side and begins the next hand.

All the players get rid of their cards until eventually there's only one player left. That's the loser. In competitive games, they'll forfeit money or some other stake, agreed before the game has started.

This hand illustrates the power of suits. The 8, 9 and 10 of spades beats the 4, 5 and 6 of spades because the sequence is made of higher cards; however, this is then beaten by the 8, 9 and 10 of hearts because hearts are more valuable than spades.

Game
Freecell

Number of players: 1
Cards used: 52
Difficulty: 6
Also known as: Patience, Solitaire

Objective
To create a sequential pile of each suit, starting with the ace.

How To Play
Another game that owes much of its popularity to the personal computer, a version of Freecell has been included with Microsoft Windows since 1995.

Deal out eight cards in a row, face up. Next, starting from the first card, lay further cards on them face up, overlapping so each is visible, until you have no more left. You'll end up with four columns of seven and four columns of six. The aim of the game is to create four sequential piles above these, one for each suit, with the ace on the bottom and finishing with the king on top.

Start by moving those aces that are at the bottom of any of the eight piles up to the top to start the get-out sequence. Continue by moving cards from one of the eight piles to another, one at a time, so the columns form a descending sequence, alternating between red and black suits. The idea is to move the aces, then 2s, then 3s, 4s, 5s and so on, to

the bottom of each pile so they can be released to the top piles. At any point in the game you can temporarily remove up to four cards – but no more – into a separate reserve to help free up new sequences in the columns. As columns are combined, you can start a new sequence by placing any card in the gap left behind. You can never have more than eight columns, though.

Variation: Original Freecell
As above, except that cards must run in suit as well as in sequence in the eight piles. While Freecell is a six on our difficulty scale, this is much harder....

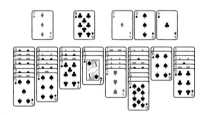

Unlike the version shipped with millions of home computers, Freecell only allows you to move a single card at a time, rather than sequences of cards, making it rather harder to win.

Game
Michigan

Number of players: 3–5
Cards used: 52
Difficulty: 4
Also known as: Newmarket, Stops

Objective

To win chips by following suits in sequence, ace high.

How To Play

Borrow an ace, king, queen and jack, all of different suits from another pack or find another way of representing them to make the 'boodle'. Each player then places a single chip on each boodle card, while the dealer places two.

Deal all the cards, including one more hand than there are players; it doesn't matter if the hands are uneven. The first player puts down the lowest card of any suit, and everyone puts their own cards in front of them, rather than on a central pile. The person with the next highest card in that suit puts it

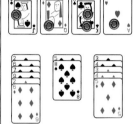

Play has been stopped twice – once by the 9 of spades and once by the 6 of diamonds.

down, then the next and so on until no one has the next highest card or until the ace is laid. This final card is called the 'stop card' and whoever lays it, simply begins with a new lowest card in the suit of their choice. There are no turns as such in Michigan – players lay cards when they're able to – and if you hold the next few cards in a sequence, you can lay them one after the other.

Lay down any of the cards in the boodle to pick up the chips there, otherwise the game ends when one player has no cards left – everyone else pays them one chip for every card they still hold.

Variation:
Pink Nines

- ♣ Everyone pays an agreed stake and the cards are dealt.
- ♣ Follow in sequence, ace low – it's the sequence that matters, not the suit.
- ♣ First player lays their longest sequence, the next player carries it on if he can, if not the turn passes to the next.
- ♣ The last person to lay a card in the sequence, starts again.
- ♣ 9s of diamonds and hearts are wild.
- ♣ The first person to run out of cards wins.

Game
Poker

Number of players: 4+
Cards used: 52
Difficulty: 5
Also known as: Five-Card Draw

Objective
To win the pot by having the highest hand, or by having people think you do.

How To Play
Poker is divided into two parts. First, there's the game itself, which features a selection of hands in ranking order.

Then, there's the bidding whereby the players add bets into a central pot to be won by the highest hand (assuming the real highest hand hasn't been cajoled into folding early, leaving a weaker hand behind to win). Both the bidding and the play progress in different ways depending on which version you play.

From botton to top, low to high, the first four hands of poker – we've left out the high card, which is the lowest – a pair, two pairs, three of a kind and a straight.

From bottom to top, from low to high the next four hands of poker: a flush, a full house, four of a kind and a straight flush. Note that some variations make 10, jack, queen, king, ace of the same suit a separate hand and call it a 'royal flush'.

Hands In Poker

From low to high, the hands in poker go like this:

♣ *High card – this is the low-rent end of the neighbourhood. If no other player has a pair, then the highest card wins the hand. In the event of a tie, you look to see what the second-highest card is, then the third and so on until someone wins.*

♣ *Pair – two of a kind beats a high card; if two players have a pair, the highest wins; in a tie, look for the highest of their remaining three cards.*

♣ *Two pairs – beat a high card and a pair with two sets of pairs; resolve any ties as described above.*

♣ *Three of a kind – three cards of the same value, together with two different cards; resolve any ties as before.*

♣ *Straight – five cards of any suit, in order; for example, 4, 5, 6, 7, 8; aces can be low or high but not both (in other words you can't have queen, king, ace, 2, 3); if more than one player has a straight, the one that includes the highest card wins; in a dead tie, the tied players split what's in the pot.*

♣ *Flush – five cards in any order that are all the same suit; highest card wins if two players have a flush.*

♣ *Full house – three of a kind and a pair; for example, three queens and two 10s. In a tie, the highest three of a kind wins, so three kings and two 2s beats three queens and two 10s; if both threes are the same (which can happen if you use wild cards), then the highest pair wins.*

♣ *Four of a kind – four cards of the same value; highest card wins a tie.*

♣ *Straight flush – five cards, in order, all of the same suit; aces can be counted high or low but not both.*

We'll describe one of the most popular, basic versions of poker here – Five-Card Draw. There's no funny scoring in poker and no suit is higher than another. Cards are ranked ace high, each player gets five cards and the highest hand wins the pot. Because poker is a gambling game, decide first of all what you're playing for. You can use anything you like so long as everyone agrees; if you use tokens, make it clear what each one stands for. Part of this is deciding what the initial bet, or ante, is going to be. Then, before the deal, each players must 'ante up', that is, pay to play that hand.

Deal five cards out to each player. Starting with the player to the dealer's left, each person will either 'call', 'raise' or 'fold' (see Betting 101, on page 62). After that, each person in the game can get rid of between one and three cards – which are put to one side – and receive the same number of new cards from the dealer.

Then the bet goes round again. After that, those players who are still in the game show their hands and the person with the highest hand wins (see 'Hands In Poker', above).

Game

Poker (continued)

How Easy?

So how come we've given poker a difficulty rating of only 5/10? Because actually, it's a pretty easy game to learn and play, especially if you're playing the basic version as described here. However, if we were rating games on how hard they are to play *well* then the score would be much higher – more like 8/10 or 9/10. Plenty of people fancy themselves as good poker players. Very few of them actually are.

Poker Shuffling

There's etiquette here that should be observed properly, even if there's only pride rather than money involved.

♣ Always shuffle and cut the deck before each hand.
♣ When the previous hand is finished, the existing dealer adds any discarded cards and squares the deck, then passes it to the player on the left of the new dealer.
♣ They shuffle the cards a minimum of four times and then give the pack to the new dealer.
♣ They pass the pack to the previous dealer who cuts it once before returning it to the new dealer.
♣ And then you're good to go.

Betting 101

After you 'ante up', there are three types of bet you can make:

♣ *Call – this means you raise your bid enough to match the stake of the person who has just bet.*
♣ *Raise – first you call the previous person's bet to match it and then you raise the bet by a specific amount (players agree bet limits before the game starts).*
♣ *Fold – this means you give up, bet nothing, and put your hand face down on the table (making sure no one sees your cards) and sit out the rest of the game; you don't have to call or raise the previous player.*

If you play the wild-card variation, you can score high hands such as this: five of a kind.

Variations

Poker's worth a book to itself. Rather than look at any of the many popular variations like Texas Hold 'em or Stud Poker, here are a few general variations that you can add to most types of poker to make the game more enjoyable.

♣ Wild cards – adding one or more wild cards to a game increases the chances of more people getting higher hands; add one or two jokers or pick an agreed card before play starts that can act as any card in any suit; for example, 2s.

♣ Spit Poker – deal four cards to each player and then add a single fifth card in the centre of the table, face up; players then count this card – traditionally known as a 'spit in the ocean' – as their own card and use it in conjunction with the four cards in their hand.

♣ Dealer's Choice – before each hand is played, the dealer specifies what kind of poker is to be played.

♣ Reduced-Pack Poker – same rules, just with a smaller pack; play with either 32 or 40 cards.

A typical hand of Five-Card Draw. Clockwise from bottom left: player one looks set to keep the two jacks and hold onto the ace; player two will keep both 10s – obviously not realizing the remaining two are held in other hands; player three will keep their spades; and player four will hold onto their 8s.

After the draw: player one has two pairs; player two has only a pair; player three nearly has a flush; and player four has three of a kind, which wins the game.

Game
Slapjack

Number of players: 2+
Cards used: 52
Difficulty: 3
Also known as: British Slapjack, Slaps

Objective
To win all the cards in the pack.

How To Play
Deal the cards out face down to each player until they're all gone. Nobody looks at their cards in Slapjack, ever. Starting from the dealer's left, the first person lays a card from the top of their hand, face up without looking at it first. (See the illustrations for how to do this.)

As soon as someone lays a jack, you have to slap your hand down on it to win the hand. Whoever gets there first picks up the pile, shuffles it into their existing hand and then starts again. If you lose all your cards, you can still continue to try and slap any jacks that appear and re-enter the game. If you slap another card by mistake, you have to give your top card to the person who went before you. The player who ends up with all the cards, and probably a sore hand, wins.

Variations
- ♣ Instead of slapping the card with the palm of your hand, use your elbow.
- ♣ A step harder: instead of slapping the card with the palm of your hand,

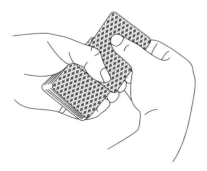

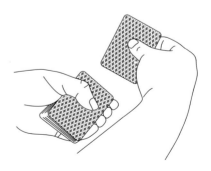

How to unveil your card: 1   *How to unveil your card: 2*

use your elbow, but keep your hand behind your back.

♣ If a player slaps the wrong card by mistake they must move their hand further away from the pile; do it again and their hand must go on their lap; do it again and they must put their hand behind their back.

Variation: British Slapjack

Set the game up in the same way. When play starts, the first person lays down their card face up in the middle and says 'ace'. The next player lays down their card and says 'two', followed by the next player who says 'three'. Cards continue to be called as they're laid down: 4, 5, 6, 7, 8, 9, 10, jack, queen, king, ace, 2 and so on – irrespective of what the face value of the card actually is. Then, if the card being laid is the same as the name of the card being spoken (in other words, as someone lays a 3 down when they say 'three') then you have to slap the card. The last person to slap – the one with their hand on the top – loses the

hand and has to pick up all the cards. If someone slaps the wrong card, they have to pick up all the cards.

Play continues until only one person has any cards. They're the loser. As an alternative, keep the counting system as described above but add an extra play – what's called 'one up, one down'. If the card you play is one higher or one lower than the value of the card you call as you lay it down, then you can also slap the pack. As before, if you get either of these wrong you have to pick up the entire pile.

Tactics

Play it fast. It's furious and fun and more players make mistakes – the way a game like this should be played. It's worth knowing that some sources define a slapjack as a sack containing one or more heavy objects, used by cut-purses in old London to knock their victims out before relieving them of their cash – so be careful when things get too frantic!

How to unveil your card: 3

How to unveil your card: 4

Game

Rummy

Number of players: 2–6
Cards used: 52
Difficulty: 5
Also known as: Gin, 500 Rum

Objective

To get rid of all the cards in your hand by laying them down to form 'melds' or 'books'.

How To Play

There are dozens of variations on the standard rummy game, but this is the most common. Each player gets seven cards. The rest of the pack goes into the middle and the dealer turns the top card over and places it beside the deck. Each player then spends a few moments trying to organize their hand into melds. A meld can be three cards of the same kind, four cards of the same kind, or a run of three or more cards of the same suit in sequence; for example, the 5, 6 and 7 of spades, or the 9, 10, jack and queen of clubs.

The player to the dealer's left starts by either picking up the first face-up card next to the pack or by drawing one from the top. If they can make one or more melds, they lay them down before returning a card to the face-up pile. Then the next player goes. The sequence is always the same – when it's your go, you pick up a card and then lay down any melds you have before discarding a card at the end of your turn.

Once you've laid down at least one meld in front of you, you can add single cards to the melds of other players in the game. Thus, for example, a typical play might go like this: pick up the 3 of hearts, add it to your existing two 3s to make a meld and lay them down; then, add an ace to someone else's run of 2, 3 and 4 of clubs before returning an unwanted 7 of spades to the pile.

The winner is the first player to get rid of all their cards by making a meld or by adding to another player's meld, or returning their final card to the upturned deck. You then add up the remaining cards held by each player and keep a running total. The highest eventual score loses the game.

Variations

There are as many variations as the day is long. Some of the most common are:
- ♣ If you want to pick up the top card of the discard pile, you must pick up the entire pile.
- ♣ Add jokers to the pack as wild cards.

Part-way through a standard rummy game. Player one is collecting queens and 10s but also has a nice run going with the 8, 9, 10 of diamonds and the potential to add more. Player two has two 3s, two jacks and two kings.

Further on in the game and player one has laid down two melds: 8, 9, 10 of diamonds and three queens, leaving him with just the 10 of clubs. Player two has laid down three 3s and is about to pick up the king to make three kings. She can then lose one of her jacks, leaving her with a single card.

♣ Nominate another card – often the 2 – as a wild card.
♣ Allow wild cards to be swapped out for the cards they represent; for example, one player has laid down a king, a 2 and a king to represent three kings, while a second player has two 3s and a king in his hand; assuming the second player has already laid down at least one meld, he may swap his king for the 2 and use that to make three 3s.
♣ The discard variation is one of the most fun – you cannot win the game by merely laying down a meld or adding a card to someone else's. Your final move must be to discard your last card.

Game
Go Fish!

Number of players: 3–6
Cards used: 52
Difficulty: 2
Also known as: Authors, Fish

Objective

To be the first player to lay down all their cards.

How To Play

Each player is dealt five cards. The rest of the pack is placed face down on the table – it'll see plenty of action in a minute. The player to the dealer's left – usually called the 'eldest' – begins the game by asking one of the other players whether they have a specific card, for example, the ace of spades or the 10 of hearts. They can't ask for any old card, though, it must be something that they already have at least one card of the same rank in their hand. Thus, if you have the aces of hearts and diamonds, the queen of spades, the 8 of spades and the 9 of clubs, you can ask for any of the following:

- ♣ The ace of clubs or spades.
- ♣ The queen of hearts, clubs or diamonds.
- ♣ The 8 of hearts, diamonds or clubs.
- ♣ The 9 of hearts, diamonds or spades.

If the player has any of those cards, they have to hand it over. In return, the first player gives them a card they don't want. If the player doesn't have any of those cards, they say: 'Go fish!' and the first player must pick up a card from the pack and the turn moves to the second player. They must then choose someone else to ask for a specific card.

As the game develops, each player must try to put together four of a kind; for example, four queens, four 7s and so on. Completed fours form a 'book' and are laid face down on the table in front of the player who collected them.

The game ends when one of the players has no cards left. The person with the most 'books' wins the game.

Variations

There are loads of variations for Go Fish! fans to enjoy. For example:

- ♣ Books can be formed by pairs or threes instead of fours.
- ♣ Books of two or three can be laid face up and other players can add to them.
- ♣ The game doesn't end when one player has no cards left; instead, they pick up from the pack and carry on.

♣ Instead of asking for a specific card, players can say something like: 'can I have all your jacks please?'

♣ Instead of ending when one player has 'booked' all their cards, they pick up a further hand from the deck and carry on playing.

♣ Instead of ending the game when the rest of the cards run out, you carry on until all the cards have been laid as books.

♣ Instead of the player who says 'Go fish!' taking the next turn it passes to the player on their left.

Tactics

Impress on all the players that it's important to be honest, otherwise a game of Go Fish! quickly descends into chaos – and if that's what floats your boat, turn to page 54 and learn how to play Cheat. Otherwise, the only tactic that players agree on is that when you pick a new card up from the pack, you should see if anyone can help turn it into a book on your next available turn.

Variation: Authors

Instead of playing with a specific number of cards and then drawing from the deck, you just deal out as many cards as you can to each player as equally as possible – it doesn't matter if everyone doesn't have exactly the same number of cards. Then play the game the same as Go Fish!, asking for cards and turning them into books of four. You must already have a card of that value in your hand before you can ask for a card of the same rank. The game ends when all of the cards have been turned into books; the winner is the person who has made the most books.

A typical hand of Go Fish! Going clockwise round the three hands, starting on the left of the pack, these are the legal requests. Player one can ask player two for the ace of spades; player two can ask player three for the 9 of spades; player three can ask player one for the 2 of spades.

Game
Crazy Eights

Number of players: 2+
Cards used: 52 or 104
Difficulty: 3
Also known as: Crazy Aces, Nines, Crates, Switch

Objective
To get rid of all the cards in your hand.

How To Play
Two to five players can play with a single pack – deal seven cards each for a two-player game and five each if more people are playing. Put the remaining cards in the middle face down, and then turn the top one over. If it's an 8, put it back in the pack, re-shuffle and try again.

Starting with the person to the dealer's left, each player must match either the suit or the rank of the upturned card – if it's the king of spades, she can play any king or any spade, if it's the 10 of hearts, any 10 or any heart. Thus a game could run like this: the 5 of spades, the 5 of hearts, the king of hearts, the 2 of hearts, the 2 of clubs and so on. 8s are wild, which means that whoever lays an 8 can tell the next player which suit they must follow with.

You don't have to take a turn if you don't want to – perhaps you're holding onto an 8 – but if you don't lay a card, you must pick up from the deck until you're able to, or until you choose to. If the deck runs out and you can't go, you must pass until you can or the game's won by someone else. The winner is the player who lays down their last card first. You then count the value of the cards left in the other players' hands – face cards are worth ten

The ace of spades was turned up, so player one followed with a jack of spades, player two laid a jack of diamonds, player one a queen of the same suit, player two a 7 of diamonds; player one has no diamonds, but can lay the 8 of spades and then tell player two which suit she must follow with.

points, suit cards carry the equivalent of their value while 8s are worth 50 points. Set a target depending on the number of players in the game; the player left standing when everyone else has reached it wins the game.

Tactics

Although it's always tempting to keep something up your sleeve, hang onto any 8s at your peril – yes, they're great cards to have, but for each one you hold at the end you'll get walloped for 50 penalty points.

Here, the game proceeds thus: jack of hearts, ace of hearts, 3 and then the king. The bottom player is about to play a 2 of hearts. Some variations say that his opponent must follow with a 2 or pick up two from the deck.

Variations

There are plenty of ways to make a game of Crazy Eights even crazier; for example, by:

- ♣ Insisting that a player continues to take a card from the pack until they find one they can play.
- ♣ Insisting that players draw a card whether they want to or not.
- ♣ Insisting that players may only draw a card if they can't lay a card from their existing hand.
- ♣ You must say 'last card' when you're down to your final card or pay a pre-agreed penalty in points or by picking up cards from the deck.
- ♣ You can lay an 8 only if it's the same suit as the previous card, in other words, an 8 of spades on a spade.
- ♣ When you play an 8 the next player must match its suit, rather than being told by you which suit to play.
- ♣ When you play a jack of any suit the next person automatically misses their go.
- ♣ When you play a queen of any suit, play changes direction.
- ♣ When someone lays a 2, the next player must match it with another 2 or take two cards from the pack; if they're able to, the next player must either lay two 2s or draw four cards from the pack and so on.

Game
Basra

Number of players: 2–4
Cards used: 52
Difficulty: 4
Also known as: Fish, Bastra, Ashush

Objective
To have the highest number of points when the last trick is won.

How To Play
Shuffle the pack and deal out four cards to each player, face down. Place a further four cards in the middle, face up. If any of these cards is a jack or the 7 of diamonds, put them back in the pack, re-shuffle and replace them.

The player to the dealer's left starts by looking at the cards in the middle and then checking their hand. They're trying to win tricks from the four face-up cards as follows:

♣ Matching any of the cards there; for example, a queen with a queen or a 10 with a 10.
♣ Laying a card that's the sum of two more of the face-up cards; for example, if there's a 5, a 4 and a 9 there, laying a 9 will capture all three cards by matching the 9 and acting as the sum of 4 and 5.

If you can't win a trick, you still play a card face up in the middle and it's the next person's turn. Whoever loses the trick lays the first card of the next hand. As the game progresses and each person lays down the last of their four cards, they are dealt another four from the pack until no more cards are left.

Each card – including the one you lay to win the trick – is worth one point, except for kings and queens, which are worth nothing. Kings and queens can only be captured by other kings and queens or by a jack or the 7 of diamonds, which wins all of the face-up cards. Clearing all of the current face-up cards with a card that's not a jack or a 7 of diamonds is a 'basra' and is worth an additional ten points. It's possible to score a basra with the 7 of diamonds, but only if the face-up cards are all numerals and add up to less than 10.

When there are no more cards left in the pack, any remaining face-up cards are taken by the player who won the last hand.

Tactics
Count those cards! As the game proceeds it becomes more and more

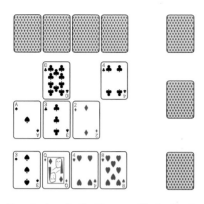

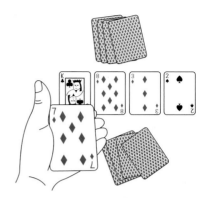

Here laying the 8 of hearts will win the 4, the 3 and the ace because together they add up to eight.

The start of a game of Basra with four cards dealt to each player and then four played face up in the middle. In some variations, the deck is then turned to reveal the bottom card – in this case it's the most powerful card in the game – the 7 of diamonds.

possible to second guess what cards the other players hold and play your hand accordingly. Basra aficionados have also developed a way of playing where they never stop moving, either playing or rearranging their cards, or demanding more cards from the dealer; this is seen particularly in the street cafés of Middle Eastern towns where the game is hugely popular. It's a great way of putting off your opponent.

Variations

Try these alternatives to spice up your game of Basra:

♣ Capturing a single jack with another jack counts as a double basra and is worth a whopping 20 points.

♣ Playing the 7 of diamonds also counts as a basra if the total value of the cards on the table is nine or less.

♣ Playing a 7 of diamonds counts as a basra when the cards you win can be split into groups that, when totalled, come to the same amount – for example, if you take a 3, 4, 2 and 5, because both the 3 and the 4 and the 2 and 5 add up to seven.

♣ Playing a 7 of diamonds counts as a basra when the cards being captured are only 10s, queens and kings of any suit.

♣ After the first hand has been dealt, the dealer turns the pack over to show both players the bottom card.

Game

Bridge

Number of players: 4 (in pairs)
Cards used: 52
Difficulty: 9
Also known as: Contract Bridge, Rubber Bridge

Objective

Winning tricks and making contracts.

How To Play

Like some of the other games included in this book, playing bridge is the easy bit – it's everything else that makes your head spin. Still, it's perfectly possible to get started without having to become an expert, though bridge aficionados should probably close their eyes now. Then, with the basics in place, the more you learn about the subtleties of bidding and the nuances of partnerships, the richer the game becomes, which is why it's one of the most enduring and enjoyable of all card games.

Rubber Bridge, hereafter just plain Bridge, uses a standard 52-card deck with the cards ranked in order from ace high down to 2. Each player picks a partner and sits opposite them, playing together against the two others. After shuffling, the dealer deals out 13 cards to each player and the game begins.

Bridge is very much like Whist, except you play in a partnership with another player, and there's bidding before the play, where you say what you're going to do. Then, the pair of players who say they can do the most get a chance to prove it, by actually playing out the hand.

During the bidding or 'auction' phase of each hand, players take it in turn to bid and say what their partnership will achieve during play. Bidding proceeds clockwise around the table starting with the dealer. When it's their turn, a player

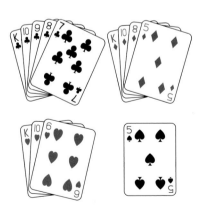

In bidding, suits take priority (low to high) in this order: clubs, diamonds, hearts and spades. Here's a typical hand.

Beginners should use a simple points system when assessing the strength or weakness of their hand before bidding. Ace is worth four, a king worth three, a queen worth two and a jack is worth one.

may choose either to bid or to pass (to register a 'no bid').

During the bidding, the suits are ranked as follows from low to high: clubs, diamonds, hearts, spades, then a 'no-trump' bid, which contracts to win tricks without declaring trumps.

Bidders may bid from the lowest bid of 'one club' (the player will make seven tricks with clubs as trumps), up to 'seven no trumps' (the player will make all 13 tricks with no suit as trumps). Notice that every bid already assumes you'll win six tricks, plus whatever your bid is.

During the auction each player must either pass or go higher than the preceding bid. If they're unable to bid at the same level as the previous bid, because of suit priority, they must bid at the next level (meaning that they bid to make one more trick). So in order to bid hearts after a 'one spade' bid, the bidder must bid at least 'two hearts'.

At any point in the auction, on their turn to bid, if a player feels that their opponents have made a bid they can't fulfil, then the player can bid 'double', doubling the points to be won or lost on that round. The other partnership may then 'redouble', quadrupling the points to be won or lost.

If no one's able to bid – if there are four consecutive 'no bids' at the start of the auction – then the hand is scrapped and the cards reshuffled and redealt.

The 'auction' ends when there are three consecutive 'no bid' responses and is won by the partnership that made the last true bid (in other words, not 'double' or 'redouble') and their bid becomes the contract that is then played out. If, for example, the final bid is 'four hearts' then the winning partnership must make ten tricks with hearts as trumps.

Most Bridge players use some kind of formalized system to help them decide how to bid, based on what cards they hold. Common systems include 'Acol' and 'Standard American'. The idea may sound off-putting, but these systems do work. They are also based on some very simple concepts.

Getting Started

Beginners should use this simple point system to help them assess the strength of their hand: an ace is worth four, a king three, queen two and jack one. (At no stage in the game do these points actually count for anything; they merely provide a framework for bidding that everyone understands and agrees to.)

Game
Bridge (continued)

Ordinarily, players will never open the bidding for their partnership unless they have at least 12 or 13 points in their hand.

If their partner has already opened the bidding for the partnership then a player may enter the bidding with fewer points – typically seven to bid a different suit or five if they simply wish to re-bid their partner's suit at the next level.

After the auction, the hand will be played by the person in the winning partnership who bid the winning suit (or 'no trumps') first. This person is called the 'declarer' and their partner is the 'dummy'. The player to the declarer's left plays their first card, which can be any card they like. The dummy then turns over their hand and lays the cards out, arranged in suits and in order in four rows so that the trump suit is on the dummy's right. From now on, the declarer plays both their own hand and the dummy's hand – in fact, the dummy can go and make refreshments for everyone. Play proceeds clockwise with players following suit when they can, and discarding or trumping when it suits their bid. As tricks are won, they should be laid face down in front of one of the partners arranged clearly so that both sides can easily see how many tricks each partnership has won. At the end of the hand, you check to see whether the declarer has made their contract by winning at least the number of tricks that they promised during the auction.

Scoring Rubber Bridge is an art in itself. Beginners would be well advised to let an experienced friend do the scoring so they focus on enjoying the game. If that's not possible then just keep score of who has won the most contracts. The attraction and entertainment of the game is the bidding and play – not the scoring!

If you do want to score properly, then check out page 79, where there's a breakdown of the scores. To make your own score sheet, get a piece of paper and draw out the grid below.

Scores for contracts successfully bid

We	*They*

Here's a typical Bridge score sheet.

Assessing Your Hand

The most important thing to remember is that you're playing with a partner. As well as thinking about your own hand, you need to put yourself in their shoes. So here are a few tips that beginners may find useful:

Bidding

♣ Ending up in the best situation – finding the best contract to be in or the best contract to leave your opponents in – is dependent on the quality of the information you and your partner are able to communicate during bidding.

♣ Each time before you bid, think about how it is likely to be interpreted by your partner. Suits aside, start as low as you can to allow time in the bidding to learn as much as possible about your partner's hand.

♣ Listen to what your partner's bids are telling you and listen to what your opponent's bids are telling you.

♣ Stick exactly to the rules of the bidding system you are using – no matter how tempting it may seem at the time, don't open or respond with one too few points, or one too few cards in a suit.

♣ If your partner opens the bidding, then they are usually in 'control'. They should choose the final contract. As responder, your role is to provide as much useful information as you can during the bidding to help them make that choice. (The exception to this rule is if you, too, have an opening hand.)

♣ Don't bid unless you can – it is just as important to know when not to bid as to know when to bid.

♣ Don't try to help your partner out by bidding more than your hand allows, no matter how tempting it may seem. That way lies disaster!

♣ Try to let your bids explain the possibilities of your hand. For example, simply re-bidding your partner's suit at the next available level communicates very little about your hand apart from its weakness.

Play

♣ As a general rule, whether you're playing or defending a contract, don't take your winning cards first. (The rare exception may sometimes, but not always, be where you have everything you need to make the contract between your two hands at the start of the play.)

♣ Usually it is better to think in terms of what you are missing – what important cards your partnership doesn't hold – and how to get those cards to fall in a way that is most helpful to you.

♣ If you are playing a contract, take a moment after the dummy lays down their hand. Think about how you are going to play the hand, and what your strategy for doing so is going to be. Don't start playing and try to work it out as you go along.

♣ If you are playing a contract, take out all the trumps early, if you believe you can. If you believe you can't then you must decide at the start whether you still want to do so or not.

♣ If you are defending a contract, the first card led, before the dummy lays down their cards, is often critical to how the play proceeds. It is usually better to lead a low card that may help your partner – based on what you know of their hand from the bidding – than it is to lead a card useful in developing your own hand. The same is often true at other times when defenders have to lead.

Game

Bridge (continued)

Duplicate Bridge

Rubber Bridge is not the only form of Bridge that is popularly played. Many people also play Duplicate Bridge.

Duplicate Bridge has exactly the same bidding and play as Rubber Bridge, but the scoring system is fundamentally different. In Rubber Bridge, the luck of the cards in the deal will influence who wins or loses. Duplicate Bridge removes that element of chance.

Duplicate requires a minimum of four pairs of players, but often involves many more. Cards are provided pre-dealt in four-slot holders. During play the cards from the hands are retained separately after play and returned as before to their holders for the next table to play.

By rotating card sets in this way each of the partnerships will bid and play every hand, and the scoring system in Duplicate Bridge means that each partnership's performance on each of the same hands can be directly measured in comparison with the other teams playing in the room.

For this reason, Duplicate Bridge is the competitive end of the sport played by Bridge clubs and used in regional, national and international competition.

and made are entered below the second horizontal line. These are called 'below the line' scores. Penalty points awarded to the opposing partnership for a failure to achieve the agreed contract, points for any overtricks (making more tricks than were actually bid), as well as other bonus and penalty scores are entered above it. These are called 'above the line scores'.

The objective is to win a rubber – which is comprised of three games. To win a game, your pair must be the first to score 100 points or more below the line. A contract bid, and made, of at least three no trumps, four hearts or four spades, or five diamonds or five clubs will yield 100 points. Alternatively, two or more lesser contracts may be required to reach 100 points. Pairs that have won one game of the rubber are designated vulnerable and attract extra bonus or penalty points, while partnerships that haven't are designated not vulnerable.

While the 'above the line' scores aren't included when it comes to working out who's won individual games, at the end of the entire rubber, all the scores are added up both above and below the line from the different games to determine which partnership has won the rubber. It's possible for a partnership to lose a rubber while winning the most games.

Contract Bridge – International Scoring

Trick Score ~ Below The Line	For each trick bid and made	Undoubled	Doubled	Redoubled
	in clubs and diamonds	20	40	80
	in hearts and spades	30	60	120
	in no trumps: the first trick	40	80	160
	following tricks	30	60	120

A game is won by 100 points below the line. The rubber is the best of three games.

Premium and Penalty Score ~ Above The Line

	Not Vulnerable			Vulnerable		
	Undoubled	Doubled	Redoubled	Undoubled	Doubled	Redoubled
Penalties						
1 undertrick	50	100	200	100	200	400
2 undertricks	100	300	600	200	500	1000
3 undertricks	150	500	1000	300	800	1600
4 undertricks	200	800	1600	400	1100	2200
5 undertricks	300	1400	2200	500	1400	2800
6 undertricks	300	1400	2800	600	1700	3400
7 undertricks	350	1700	3400	700	2000	4000
Premiums Each overtrick	Trick value	100	200	Trick value	200	400
For making a doubled or redoubled contract	N/A	50	100	N/A	50	50
Slam bid score — Small			500	750		
Slam bid score — Grand			1000	1500		
Rubber bonus score	In two games 700		In three games 500	Unfinished rubber, for one game 300	Unfinished rubber, for one game 100	
Trump honours in the same hand ace king, queen, jack, 10	Four 100		Five 150	For aces in no. trumps 150		

Game
Bstrideridge (continued)

Bridge (continued)

An Example Hand

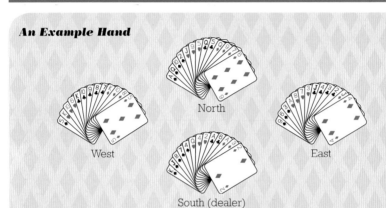

North

West

East

South (dealer)

Player	Bid	Explanation
South	(Bids first, as dealer) Opens ' one spade.'	Shows 12–13 points and at least four spade cards.
West	No bid.	Not enough points to open.
North	Responds with 'two diamonds'.	Shows at least seven points and at least a four-card diamond suit. It is better and stronger to bid the diamonds than the spades, because it opens up more possibilities for the bidding. Bidding spades at this point would almost certainly lead to a spade contract.
East	No bid.	Not enough points to open.
South	'Two no trumps'.	Shows no particular preference for playing diamonds and indicates individual strong cards in clubs and hearts.
West	No bid.	
North	'Four spades'.	North takes the decision to play in spades rather than no trumps. The bid finally indicates both North's additional points and also the strength in partner's preferred suit.

So South, as the partner in the winning pair that first bid spades, will play the hand with spades as trumps, needing to win ten tricks to fulfil North's contract of 'four spades'.

Game
Chase the Ace

Number of players: 3+
Cards used: 52
Difficulty: 3
Also known as: Cuckoo, Screw Your Neighbour, Ranter Go Round

Objective
To have the highest card at the end of each hand.

How To Play
Decide how many lives each player gets, then put a stake in a pot. The dealer deals a single card to each player, who then looks at it and decides whether or not to keep it, or swap it with the person to their left – the idea is to be the one who has the highest card at the end of the round. No one can refuse an exchange unless they have a king, in

which case they have to turn it face up. The dealer doesn't swap with another player; instead he can keep his card or swap it for one from the pack. After the dealer's turn, everyone turns over their cards and whoever has the lowest card loses a life; tied players all lose a life. Kings are high, aces are low.

Variation: Cuckoo
A player says 'cuckoo' when they won't swap because they have a king; if they have a jack they can refuse a trade and you must swap with the next player along.

Here's a five-player hand with the dealer's 5 of spades at the bottom. Of course, in a real game, these cards wouldn't be displayed face up.

The 10 swaps with the ace. The ace can't swap with the king. The player with the jack keeps it. The dealer cuts and replaces his 5. The player with the ace loses a life.

Game
Botifarra

Number of players: 4
Cards used: 48
Difficulty: 6

Objective

To take tricks and win points, usually first to 101.

How To Play

One of the interesting things about this Catalan game is that it's played with a special deck. You can find Spanish decks online or make one yourself by simply removing the 10s from the pack. Cards rank as follows: 9, ace, king, queen

Dealer is to the south and has a good enough hand to bet no trumps. Player to the dealer's right (remember that Botifarra is played anticlockwise) bids 'contrar' to double the score and the dealer's partner then bids 'recontrar' to double it again. No other bids are made.

(called the 'horse' in a Spanish deck), jack, 8, 7, 6, 5, 4, 3, 2.

Botifarra is a trick-taking game played by four people in two pairs who sit opposite each other, like in Bridge. Highest cut deals the cards four at a time until all the cards have been used. The deal, passing the deal, bidding and the play all happen anticlockwise, which is the first thing you'll have to get used to.

Everyone looks at their cards, which are scored as follows: 9 (five points), ace (four points), king (three), queen (two), jack (one); in addition, each winning trick is worth a point. Dealer picks trumps or 'Botifarra' (no trumps) or passes, at which point her partner must choose instead – she cannot pass. The points in no-trump games are automatically doubled.

Having chosen trumps, the bidding begins. The non-dealing partnership can bid 'contrar' to double the hand, and the dealer's partnership can then bid 'recontrar' to double it again; if the other partnership is really confident, they can bid 'Sant Vicens' to double it again.

The dealer then plays their first card and the player to their right follows. You must follow suit if you can, and if your partner isn't winning the current trick and you are able to, you must lay a card strong enough to do so. If your partner is already winning the trick there are only certain cards you can lay – either a 9, ace, king, queen or jack, or the lowest card you hold in whichever suit you choose to play. If the other partnership's winning the trick, they have to play the lowest card you hold in whichever suit you play. There's one exception to this: if you're playing the second card in the trick and can't follow suit you are allowed to play a 9, ace, king, queen or jack.

At the end of each hand, each pair adds up their score, counting a point for each trick and extra points depending on which cards they've captured –

The end of the hand: the dealer's pair has won nine tricks and their opponents three. The dealer's point-scoring cards are laid out in the bottom two rows and count for 45; the other pair scores five. Dealer wins by 54 to 8, but also bid 'recontrar', which quadruples that to 216.

remember that 9s are the highest card, followed by aces, kings and so on (see earlier for the points that each card scores). Remember to take into account any hands that have been doubled or redoubled.

Variations

Try these for a slightly different game of Botifarra:

- ♣ For a faster, easier game that's less tactical, omit this rule entirely: 'If your partner is already winning the trick there are only certain cards you can lay – either a 9, ace, king, queen or jack, or the lowest card you hold in whichever suit you choose to play.'
- ♣ It's also possible to extend the exception for the second player so that it also applies when they are able to follow suit – they can play a 9, ace, king, queen or jack.
- ♣ There's also an interesting scoring variation that allows partnerships to carry over any score they make that's more than 101 to the next game; alternatively, you can play that only the winning partnership gets to do this and the losers carry over nothing.

Game
Tax Collector

Number of players: 3–7
Cards used: 45
Difficulty: 2
Also known as: Farmer

Objective

To collect cards and get as close to 16 as possible, but no higher!

How To Play

Decide what you're going to use for chips – in this example we'll use pennies. Start by taking out all the 8s and the 6 of clubs, spades and diamonds – leaving the 6 of hearts. Cut to see who deals and then give everyone a single card, face down. Everyone 'antes up' into the pool in the middle, betting a single penny, and then looks at their card. Starting with the player on the dealer's left, each player asks for at least one card, but can also request more. When they've finished making their hand, they say 'pass' and play goes round clockwise until everyone has passed. You don't have to tell any of the other players whether you've busted or not, so when everyone's passed and you all turn over your cards, it's quite likely that one or more of you in a big hand will have busted.

Whichever player has 16, or gets nearest to it without busting, wins the game and all the pennies in the pot. If two players have the same score, they split the pot.

The dealer continues until someone scores exactly 16, at which point they surrender the deal. If more than one player has 16, the dealer – the 'tax collector' – has precedence, followed by the player holding the 6 of hearts, followed by the hand with the fewest cards, followed by the player to the dealer's left.

A hand of Tax Collector. The dealer's cards are at the bottom. As you can see, both the second and third players have scored 16; in the event of a tie (and because the dealer doesn't have 16), the winner is the player with the 6 of hearts.

Game

Hearts

Number of players: 4
Cards used: 52
Difficulty: 4
Also known as: Black Maria, Dirty Lady

Objective

To avoid winning hands with hearts or the queen of spades in.

How To Play

Deal 13 cards, face down. Pick three to pass on – the aim is to avoid winning any hearts or the queen of spades. Pass to the left for the first hand, the right for the second and opposite for the third, then repeat.

The beginning of a hand where you must pass three cards to an opponent. Good choices here would be the ace of clubs, the king and ace of diamonds, the king of spades or the queen of hearts.

Whoever has the 2 of clubs starts. You must follow suit if you can, otherwise, you can lay any card; the exception is the first hand where you cannot lay a heart or the queen of spades.

At the end of each round, you score a point for each heart contained in hands that you won, while the queen of spades scores 13. The game ends when a player reaches 100; the winner is the person with the lowest score.

If you've a high hand you can try to win every trick. If you succeed, you score zero and everyone else gets 26 penalty points.

Variation: Black Maria

A variant for three players: remove the two of clubs and deal 17 cards to each

Player one leads with the 4 of diamonds, player two follows with the 7, player three can't follow suit so lays the queen of spades, and player four lays the 10 of hearts. Unlucky player two wins the trick and 14 penalty points.

player. The three cards are always passed left and the first player can start with any card. Penalty points are also different: each heart scores a point and the queen of spades 13, the king and ace of spades attract penalties of ten and seven respectively. If you win every trick, you score zero and everyone else 43.

Section 2

Skills

Skill
Wash the Deck

Difficulty: 2

Objective
To shuffle the cards on a table.

How To Do It
Kids and occasional card players can find it tricky to shuffle a deck. The result? More time spent under the table searching for escapees and less time playing on it. This is the shuffle for them.

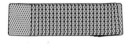

Step 1
Take the deck of cards and spread it out on a flat surface in front of you in two rows, face down.

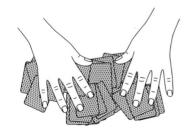

Step 2
Using both hands, push the two rows of cards together and mix them up.

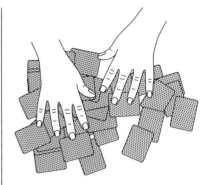

Step 3
Next, 'wash' the cards with both hands using clockwise and anticlockwise circular motions until they're as mixed up as they're going to be.

Step 4
Gather the cards together with gentle motions, being careful not to flip any of them over or you'll have to start again. Slowly square the deck up, and you're ready to start your game.

Skill
Strip Shuffle

Difficulty: 2

Objective
To shuffle the cards using both hands side to side on the table.

How To Do It
This is used in casinos and by those who fancy themselves as 'proper' players.

Step 1
Place the cards face down on the table and sideways on.

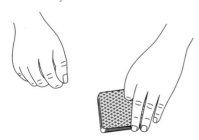

Step 2
Place your left hand over the deck with your first finger bent over so it rests lightly on the pack, as shown. Your thumb should be behind the deck and your first three fingers in front; you should be able to lift the deck slightly off the table.

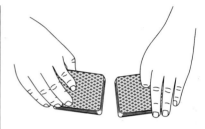

Step 3
Make the same shape with your other hand and then pinch some cards from the top of the deck and slide them to the side.

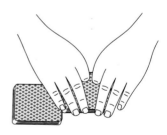

Step 4
Let the cards you've just taken drop to the table and then repeat the motion. When there are only a few cards left in the original deck, just pop these on top of the new pile to complete the shuffle.

Skill

Overhand Shuffle

Difficulty: 3

Objective

To shuffle the cards using both hands but no table, ready for a game.

How To Do It

The Overhand Shuffle is one of the classics that everyone thinks of when they picture someone shuffling a deck of cards. It's relatively simple, effective and easy to master. When you're more comfortable with it, you'll discover that you can move both hands in an easy together-apart-together-apart motion to make the shuffle much smoother.

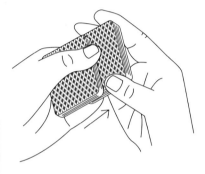

Step 2

Move your left hand up and pull some cards down toward the palm using your thumb.

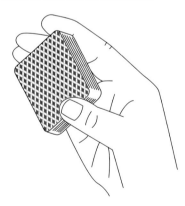

Step 1

Hold the deck in your right hand with your thumb at one end and first three fingers at the other with the cards facing your palm.

> #### Monge's Shuffle
> *Want an even easier way to shuffle cards for a game? Try Monge's Shuffle. Hold the deck face down in your left hand and then, using your thumb, pass the top card across to your right hand. Then, pass the new top card in your left hand across and place it on top of the card in your right hand. Take the new top card in your left hand and pass it across to the bottom of the cards in your right hand. Then pass the next to the top, the next to the bottom, and keep alternating top and bottom until the entire deck has been transferred from one hand to the other.*

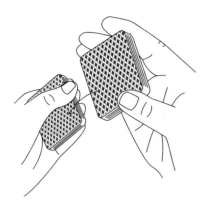

Step 3

Continue the pulling motion and at the same time lift your right hand away so that the cards drop into the palm of the other hand. Then drop some more cards on top of that.

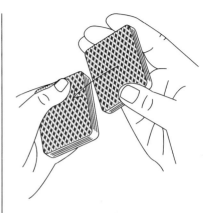

Step 5

Pull the pack out completely so that the pile of cards in your left hand is complete.

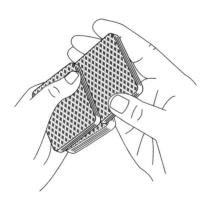

Step 4

Pull the remaining cards up – notice that they're sandwiched between the first lot of cards you pulled and the second lot that you're about to drop.

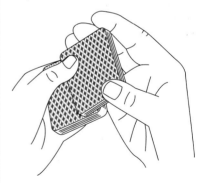

Step 6

Continue passing cards into your left hand using this drop and pull, drop and pull motion until all the cards are in your left hand and your right hand is empty. Then start again. Repeat three or four times between hands in a game of cards.

Skill
Hindu Shuffle

Difficulty: 5

Objective
To shuffle the cards using both hands without the use of a table or other flat surface; favoured by magicians.

How To Do It
As we'll see later on, the Hindu Shuffle is a favourite of magicians because it's possible to conceal an entire arsenal of fakery and fiddles behind it. In order to show how it's done more clearly, we show it side on here, rather than with the cards held portrait-style, face down as if being offered to the onlooker.

Step 1
Lightly grasp the deck of cards in your left hand – thumb at the back, first finger at the end furthest away from you and the other three fingers resting gently along the outer edge. Hold the cards quite high up, near the tops of your fingers.

Step 2
Next, grab about three quarters of the pack with your other hand and pull it away from the rest of the hand. As you pull the majority of the deck away, drop the forefinger of the other hand onto the top card to hold everything in place. At the same time, use the thumb and fingers of the left hand to pinch the remaining cards and hold them in place while you slide the others out.

Step 3
With the majority of the deck withdrawn and held in the right hand, release the remaining cards so they drop into the palm of the left hand.

Step 4
Return the majority of the deck back to your left hand and hold it again using the original grip from Step 1.

Step 5
This is the difficult bit. You have to balance the small pile of cards in the palm of your left hand, while gripping a roughly equal amount with the tops of your thumb and fingers. Then you use the right hand to withdraw the rest of the pack. After that, let the top pile drop onto the bottom pile in your left hand and repeat until you have no more cards left in your right hand.

Step 1

Step 2

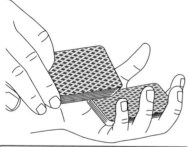

Step 3

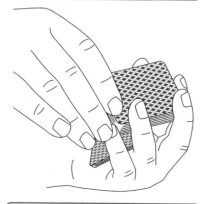

Step 4

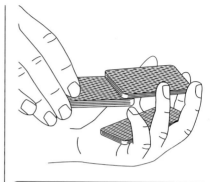

Step 5

Putting It Into Practice

In practice, most magicians use the Hindu Shuffle with the cards facing the audience, as shown in this illustration. Later in the book we'll show you why this shuffle is so useful for card trickery.

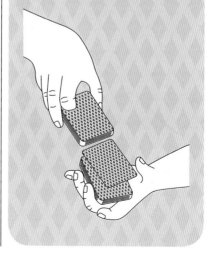

Skill
Pharaoh Shuffle

Difficulty: **6**

Objective
To shuffle the cards using both hands, without the use of a table or other flat surface, using the riffle technique.

How To Do It
This is supposedly the simplest of the riffle shuffle family, and if the Table Riffle (see pages 96–7) defeats you, it's effective enough. Like all riffles, the idea is simple: to split the deck in half and then somehow interleave the two sets of cards one over another, over another and so on. So let's have a look.

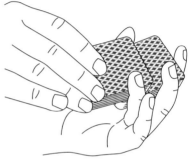

Step 2
Grip about half the pack, or as close as you can get, with your right hand, and pull it away from the rest of the deck. Don't let the remainder drop into the palm of your left hand, but keep them gripped between your fingers and thumb there.

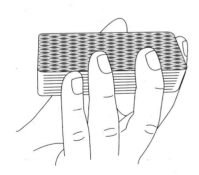

Step 1
Hold the pack in your left hand as shown above. The grip is the same as for the Hindu Shuffle – forefinger at the short end of the deck, thumb at the back, three fingers at the front, with the deck held fairly high up.

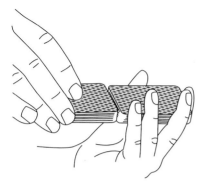

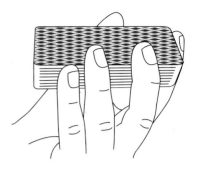

Step 3

Line the two decks up so that the edges of their shorter sides are nudging against each other. Relax the grip on each pack ever so slightly – you want the cards to have the small amount of movement necessary to make the shuffle happen, but not so much that you can't control what's going on.

Step 5

Once the two packs 'concertina' nicely, gently push them together with small side-to-side movements until the pack is integrated once again.

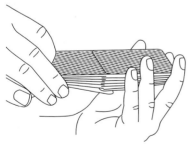

Step 4

Using short side-to-side movements, you need to try and feed one pack into the other so that the cards go over and under, over and under. This takes some practice, but persevere and you'll get the hang of it.

Tips

Some people find it difficult to get the initial 'key' between the two sets of cards. If that's the case, instead of trying to weave them together end to end, try doing it corner to corner and then rotating them inward to join the two ends.

The other mistake that beginners make is to hold the cards too loosely and too near the middle. Instead, hold them more toward the end of the deck and quite tightly. This will give you the control and the purchase you need but leave the far end of each pack – where you're trying to join them together – with the flexibility you need to make the shuffle work.

Skill
Table Riffle Shuffle

Difficulty: 4

Objective
To shuffle the cards on a table using both hands to weave them together.

How To Do It
Along with the Overhand Shuffle, and to a lesser extent the Hindu Shuffle, this is the one that people associate with card playing. It sounds good, as though the cards are really getting a good shuffle, and, if you check 'The Perfect Shuffle' box opposite, you'll find that it's one of the most effective ways to ensure that a deck is properly shuffled ready for play.

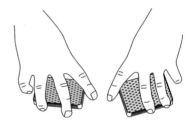

Step 2
Hold the top half of the deck with your right and the bottom half with your left and then smoothly slide the top half off and to the right, like so.

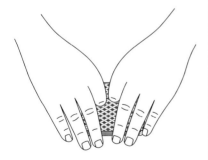

Step 1
Start with the cards face down on the table in front of you, landscape-style as shown here. Then, make sure the first fingers of both hands are bent in and grip the deck with your thumbs at the back and second and third fingers at the front.

Step 3
Square up each half of the deck if necessary and then bring in the two corners nearest to you so they're angled together. Then, lift the corners off the table with your thumbs and move them even closer together.

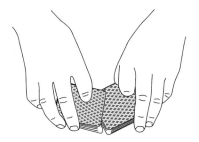

Step 4

Push down on the top of both decks with the first finger of each hand and then, with one of your thumbs, release one of the cards so it slaps down onto the table. Then release one with the other thumb. Slowly picking up speed, release cards one at a time, alternating hands so that the two decks weave together.

The Perfect Shuffle

According to research conducted by Persi Diaconis, a professor of statistics and mathematics at Stanford University in the United States, there is a point beyond which it's not worth shuffling a deck of cards any more because the randomness induced by the shuffle ceases to be significant. With the riffle, this happens after seven shuffles, which is why that's the recommended number that casinos and other gaming houses should practise. In fact, many typically only riffle a deck three times. Which makes you wonder why....

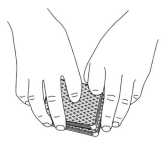

Step 5

Finally, gently push the deck together and square it up, always keeping the cards face down on the table so that none of the other players – or the audience if it's a trick – can see them. Then repeat the riffle as many times as you like.

Skill
Airborne Riffle Shuffle

Difficulty: 6

Objective
To riffle shuffle the cards using both hands to weave them together ... in the air!

How To Do It
This requires both dexterity and a certain strength in order to riffle the cards and stay in control. It's a shuffle used when there's no flat surface available – perhaps when you're camping or playing with a friend on the train – but is also used by magicians because it's noisy and a bit flashy, which everyone likes.

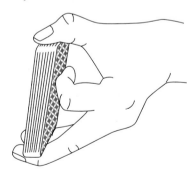

Step 1
Hold the pack in your left hand, portrait-style with the back of the cards facing your palm, thumb on the top, first finger bent behind, second and third fingers supporting the pack underneath, and the little finger resting on the long side nearest your body.

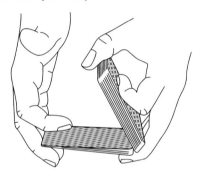

Step 2
Lean your thumb back ever so slightly and then put pressure on the back of the cards with your first finger to push about half the pack forward, away from your palm. Then, bring your other hand in and let this half drop onto the tips of your second and third fingers of your left hand, while the first finger of that hand comes over the top of the cards. At this point half the cards should be in their original position and the other half should be being held by the tips of the second and third fingers of both hands, like a little bridge.

Step 5

With the cards half joined, you can just kind of pat them in and square the deck up.

Step 3

Leaving all the cards and all your fingers as they are, simply lift your left hand up; as you do, the other half of the pack will naturally lift into position so you can grip the top with your left thumb.

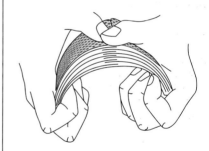

Step 6

Alternatively, you can add a flourish by holding the cards as shown here and then pushing them in and up so that the newly joined pack meshes together.

Step 4

This is where the strength and control come in. Bring both thumbs down to nearly meet in the middle and bend both halves of the pack, pushing with your first finger on the back of each one and holding them steady with the rest of your hand. Release one card from one hand and then the next from the other, and then the next from the first hand, and so on until all the cards are woven together.

Skill
Casino Shuffle

Difficulty: 4

Objective
To prepare the deck for a game of cards using a combination of techniques that's often called the Casino Shuffle.

How To Do It
This looks great. The beauty of the Casino Shuffle is that it's actually very easy, but by combining a number of different elements into a single pre-game procedure, you can look like a professional – a real dealer. All of the techniques used in this shuffle are discussed elsewhere in the book in more detail. (Note that some people refer to this as the Blackjack Shuffle because it's taught to dealers who primarily work the blackjack tables.)

Step 1
Wash the deck thoroughly as described on page 88. Be especially careful not to leave out any cards during this process – beginners sometimes leave the odd card or two outside the main wash and only bring them in at the end when they're tidying up. Seasoned card players don't like this.

Step 2
Square the cards off and then cut the deck in half once, taking the top half off and placing it in front of the other half, then taking the half closest to you and placing it on top of the rest of the cards.

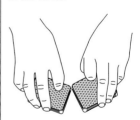

Step 3
Riffle the pack twice, using the Table Riffle Shuffle described on page 96. The important thing here

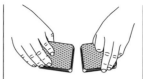
is to make sure that the last card down on the top of the pack alternates – so left first and then right.

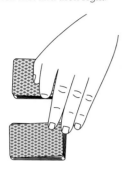

Step 4
Cut the deck again exactly as you did in Step 2.

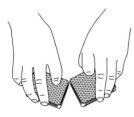

Step 5
Add two more riffle shuffles as you did in Step 3, making sure to alternate those top cards properly.

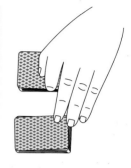

Step 6
Next, do a smooth Strip Shuffle as described on page 89, remembering to lift the deck slightly off the table to facilitate a nice easy stripping action.

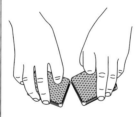

Step 7
Give the deck a final riffle. Purists will remember whether the last top card from the previous riffle was a left or a right and make sure that this final riffle alternates again; but don't expect many of your fellow card players to pick you up if you don't do this.

Step 8
Cut the cards one last time as you did in Steps 2 and 4.

Tip
With some shuffles and tricks, beginners often find that the top couple of cards take on a life of their own and slide about. Try it – just pop the deck down on the table and watch what happens. You can stop this by resting your forefinger on the top card for a moment when you set the deck down.

Skill
One-Handed Shuffle

Difficulty: 8

Objective
To shuffle the cards and show off while you're doing it.

How To Do It
A good shuffle is important – in a game of cards, for example, it's a demonstration of fairness, and in a trick it's a useful way to misdirect an audience. It's also a great way to show off, especially as it uses only one hand!

Step 1
Start by holding the deck in your left hand so that the second, third and fourth fingers are on the right-hand side. Stay relaxed.

Step 2
Slip your first finger behind the cards and push the deck up so it's held between the thumb and tips of your fingers.

Step 3
Bring the first finger out from behind the deck and use it to grip the top of the pack, then slide the little finger down to a similar position along the bottom.

Step 4
Split the deck with your index finger, as shown opposite.

Step 5
Tip your hand as shown, and lower your second and third fingers so that the top half of the pack slides away from the bottom half on the nail of your first finger (which is still between the two halves of the pack).

Step 6
Continue sliding the top half of the pack away from the bottom half until you can poke your first finger between them.

Step 7
Slide your little finger round the edge of the top pack until it's on the long side and then move the second finger round until it's on the top side.

Step 8
Slide the first finger out of the gap and as you do, push down gently with the second finger to start meshing the two decks together.

Step 9
Here's the deck being pushed together. As soon as the cards are meshed, the whole pack becomes much more stable.

Step 10
Continue pushing gently until the two halves of the pack are completely interlaced and you can push them together to complete the shuffle.

Step 1

Step 2

Step 3

Step 4

Step 5

Step 6

Tip

As with all complex moves, this requires practice. If you've got small hands, you may find it easier to start with a three-quarter-sized pack. This will enable you to get the movements right without worrying about the stretch too much. Once the shuffle is smooth, you can graduate to a full-sized pack.

Step 7

Step 8

Step 9

Step 10

Skill
Simple Cut

Difficulty: 1

Objective
To cut the deck in half so that the top half becomes the bottom half and the bottom becomes the top.

How To Do It
Cutting the deck is one of the most basic preparations for play. There are no prescribed rules as to what constitutes a cut, beyond a recognition that it should be made up of at least one quarter of the deck. It's common in casinos to either cut the pack in half or cut it in thirds; either way, it's easy to master and works like this.

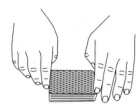

Step 1
Place the deck in front of you on the table with the long edge facing you.

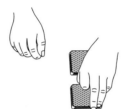

Step 2
Use your favoured hand to pick up half the deck with your second and third fingers on the edge furthest away from you, your thumb on the near edge, and your first finger bent over as shown in the illustration. Then drop the top half in front of the existing deck, remembering to keep your first finger on the top for a second after you put it down – this will stop the top cards from sliding.

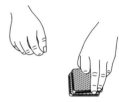

Step 3
Pick up the pile closest to you in exactly the same way and then pop it on top of the other pile. Square the deck up if necessary to complete the cut.

House Rules
In casinos, players are never allowed to cut the deck to stop them from cheating, but at home it's often considered a sign of a scrupulously fair game to allow players other than the dealer to cut the deck periodically. Remember, a fair game of cards is a happy game of cards.

Skill
Triple Cut

Difficulty: 2

Objective

To cut the deck in threes so that each third changes place during the shuffle.

How To Do It

The Triple Cut is used more by magicians than card players because of various techniques you can use to control cards and where they appear in the pack. We'll look at some of these later, but for now, let's concentrate on the mechanics of the shuffle itself.

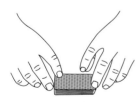

Step 1

Start by placing the deck of cards in front of you, landscape-style as shown in the illustration. What we're going to do is pull the bottom third of the deck out to the side and

then bring it round to the front and pop it on top of the pile.

Step 2

Raise the whole deck ever so slightly off the table with your left hand – first finger bent over on the top, second and third fingers at the front, and thumb at the back. Hold the cards toward one end, as shown in the illustration. Then reach in with your right hand and grab the bottom third of the deck – using the same grip – and pull it out to the side.

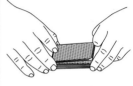

Step 3

Bring the bottom third around in front of the deck and drop it onto the top.

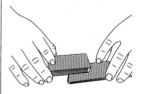

Step 4

Then repeat, this time with your left hand, taking the bottom third out from underneath, bringing it round to the front and then dropping it on top of the deck.

Skill
Air Cut

Difficulty: 4

Objective
To cut the deck in half without using a table.

How To Do It
Magicians love the Air Cut because you don't need a table. Also, if you're doing close magic at a party or in a bar, you probably don't want to use the table anyway because it'll be all sticky and mess your cards up. So this simple shuffle is definitely worth learning.

Step 1
Start with the pack in your left hand with your thumb on the corner furthest away from you, your first finger cradling the front, and the others down the side. Then, bring your right hand over the

top and get about half the pack between your second and third fingers at the front and your thumb at the back; your first finger is bent over on top of the pack as shown.

Step 2
Pick up the top half of the pack and move it over to the right of the rest of the deck and keep it there while we do some stuff with the left hand.

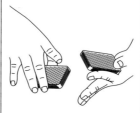

Step 3
What you want to do now is squeeze what's left of the original deck between

your left thumb and the bottom of your first finger. As you do, the other fingers of your left hand will fall away and the deck will naturally tilt forward ever so slightly.

Step 4
Bring the cards in your left hand in towards the cards in your right hand – we're going to be putting them on the top. As you do, lift the first finger of your right hand off the deck and then slide the other half in on top of it to complete the air cut.

Skill
Pivot Cut

Difficulty: 4

Objective
To cut the deck without using a flat surface.

How To Do It
Magicians like this even more than the Air Cut because it's flashier, and when mastered produces a wonderfully silky cut that at first is surprisingly difficult for the audience to work out. And anything that confuses an audience is always a good thing.

Step 1
Hold the deck in your right hand with your thumb at the back and your second and third fingers at the front. Notice that we've positioned our fingers well toward the outside edge of the pack – it'll become clear why in a moment.

Step 2
Next, use the first finger of your right hand to 'pick up' half the deck by prising it away from the bottom half, which should still be held securely by your other fingers and thumb.

Step 3
Next, you need to pivot the cards you're gripping with your first finger toward your left hand. Then bring the left hand so that you can slot the raised part of the deck in between the base of your first finger and your thumb.

Step 4
Once the cards are in position, squeeze your right first finger and thumb to hold them in place and then bring the cards in your right hand up and on top of the pile that's gripped in your left hand to complete the cut.

Skill
Air Twist and Pivot Cut

Difficulty: 2

Objective
To add a nice flourish to a straight air cut.

How To Do It
For all those times when you're performing tricks and don't have a table, the Air Twist and Pivot Cut makes you look good while performing a simple cut. The unusual second hand position – at first, some people mistakenly try to use their thumb instead of their first finger – also makes it appear more complex and therefore more thorough than it actually is. It also works well as part of a sequence of shuffles and cuts.

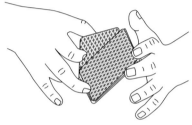

Step 2
Use the first finger of your other hand to push the back right corner of about half the deck anticlockwise away from your body.

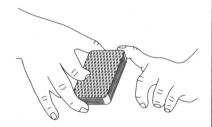

Step 1
Hold the deck face down from the top with your thumb at the back and your middle finger at the front, maybe two thirds of the way along. This leaves plenty of space for you to use the first finger of your other hand to pivot out part of the deck to start the cut.

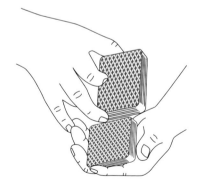

Step 3
Continue the movement forward and round – the pushing hand will naturally end up in front of the other hand, palm up, so that the top half of the deck drops into it. Pop the other half on top to finish.

Skill
Charlier Cut

Difficulty: 5

Objective
To perform an impressive one-handed cut.

How To Do It
This can also be used two-handed if you split the deck first and hold half in each hand.

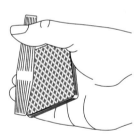

Step 1
Hold the cards with your thumb on the top and the rest of your fingers on the bottom. Get the pack as close to the tips of your fingers as is comfortable – especially if you've got smaller hands. When you're in position, lift the ball of your thumb slightly and let about half the pack drop into your palm.

Step 2
Next, use your first finger to push the cards on your palm up until they form an arch with the rest of the pack, as shown here.

Step 3
Be careful not to drop the whole lot, as you continue to push the cards that were in your palm up and over the top of the rest of the deck. The front half of the deck is now resting on

your first finger and the back half is resting on the front half.

Step 4
Move your first finger out of the way and the front half will fall onto your palm while the back half falls on top of the front half, thus completing the cut.

Skill
Spring the Deck

Difficulty: 7

Objective
To introduce a bit of razzmatazz into your magic act.

How To Do It
Let's be clear. Springing cards – where you use one hand to propel the cards through the air really quickly is very easy. Catching the cards with the other hand, is really hard. Springing serves no useful purpose and don't think for a moment that it shuffles the deck because it's got nothing to do with it. Springing is all about flash and dazzle.

Step 1
Use half the deck and don't be tempted to hold it like this, using your first finger to push the cards out. This is wrong and won't help you to spring the deck.

Step 2
Instead, hold the cards like this, bending them in toward the palm of your hand. It seems wrong, but it gives you more control. Use your thumb to feel the edges of the cards and with care you can even release them one at a time like this.

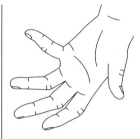

Step 3
That's actually the easy bit. The hard bit is catching them. Hold your hand like this, almost like a claw, to prevent the cards from shooting all over the table, or for that matter your audience!

Quick Fix
Still having trouble? Try holding the cards by opposite corners instead of along the short edge. This is easier on the hands and gives you more control.

Skill
Straight Deal

Difficulty: 2

Objective

To deal cards for a game quickly and efficiently, without exposing their faces to the people playing the game.

How To Do It

Surprisingly, many people can't deal cards properly. They pull off more than one at a time from the deck, they bend the cards up so anyone can see what's being dealt, and double-card (deal more than one card to a player). Here's how to do it properly.

Step 1

Hold the deck of cards face down like this with three fingers down one long side, the first finger holding the end, and the thumb on top. This gives you complete control over the cards.

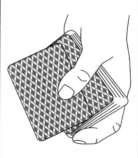

Step 2

Use your thumb to push out the top card to the side. It'll go out and up and over your three fingers; you should be able to feel that you've pushed only one card out, rather than two or three.

Step 3

Use your other hand to take the pushed card from the top of the pack by holding it toward the top corner, furthest away from you and – keeping the card angled down – lay it in front of the first player. Avoid the temptation to slap the card down, as this involves lifting the end nearest to the table; this means players may well be able to see the face of the cards.

Skill
Throw Deal

Difficulty: 4

Objective
To deal the cards one at a time to players sitting on the other side of the table.

How To Do It
When you're dealing cards, it's not cool to lean right over the table. Tossing the cards is dangerous too, because they're just as likely to land face up. Instead, use this simple method for a controlled, face-down throw every time.

Step 1
Start by looking at the straight deal on the previous page for the hand positions and then strip off the top card as shown here.

Step 2
Instead of using your finger and thumb to pull the card off the deck and deal it out, you want to pinch the card lightly between your first and second fingers, as shown here. This will allow you to use a nice easy flick and propel the cards across the table.

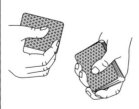

Step 3
The trick here is to let the card do the work and not to try and throw it too hard. Cards have decent aerodynamics and want to glide over surfaces like tables, so if you hook your wrist back and then flick it forward, you'll get good distance and the card won't flip over.

Step 4
And here's the final hand position shown from above with the card gripped loosely between first and second fingers, just before the release.

Skill
One-Handed Deal

Difficulty: 6

Objective
To deal the cards one at a time to players who are sitting on the other side of the table. With one hand.

How To Do It
We'll come clean here. This isn't a proper deal – the cards are too hard to control. However, it's a fun way to give players a card or two in pontoon or blackjack.

Step 1
The funny thing about this is that although we deal with our right hand, we hold the deck with our left and this feels more natural, even though it's not our favoured hand. So, hold the deck as if for dealing but with your thumb slightly further toward the front. Push a card out with your thumb, then pop your third finger under it.

Step 2
Bring your second finger over the top of the card and at the same time lift your thumb up and out of the way.

Step 3
Straighten your third finger under the card and as you do it will naturally ease round to the side where a gentle finger flick will send it off and across the table.

Step 1

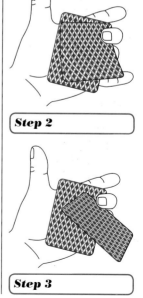

Step 2

Step 3

Skill
Strike Second Deal

Difficulty: 4

Objective

To keep the top card for yourself when dealing a hand of cards.

How To Do It

While we'd never encourage cheating your friends at cards, a simple technique like this can be useful as part of a trick. There are some more sophisticated false deals in a page or two, but we'll start here because it's the easiest and works really well, especially if you use a highly patterned deck of cards. All the better for deceiving the eye…

Step 1

Hold the deck in the standard dealing grip. Purists like this one with three fingers down the side, first finger at the front and thumb over the top, but really you can hold the deck pretty much as you like, so long as you can control the top card and get at the card underneath.

Step 2

You then need to rotate the top card, the one you want for yourself, with your thumb so that it moves away from the front of the pack and to the side you'd normally take the cards from in an ordinary deal.

Step 3

Use your other hand to take the second card in a nice smooth movement.

Step 4

As you deal each card, complete the movement by bringing the top card back over the rest of the deck with your thumb. Combining both hands in a smooth rotate-take-rotate-back movement makes it tough for an audience to spot that anything suspicious is going on.

Skill
Push-Off Second Deal

Difficulty: 7

Objective
To keep the top card for yourself when dealing.

How To Do It
This is harder than the 'strike' version on the previous page but has the advantage that, when mastered, it is even harder to detect. With a smooth action it's almost impossible for anyone watching to spot. And it's so simple that it's almost beyond suspicion.

Step 1
Decide on the card you'd like to stay at the top of the deck all the way through the deal. We've chosen the ace of spades.

Step 2
Turn it over and hold the deck like so in your left hand with your first finger at the front, three fingers down the side, and thumb wrapped over the top.

Step 3
This bit just takes practice. Using exactly the same movement as a standard,

above-board deal, use your thumb to push off the top two cards. At first it seems like you'll never get it, but like many sleights, after a while it just clicks and becomes much easier.

Step 4
Bring your other hand in and then pull the second card out from underneath the first one. At the same time, pull the top card back square onto the deck with your left thumb.

Skill
Bottom Deal

Difficulty: 8

Objective

To deal as many cards for yourself as you like off the bottom of the deck.

How To Do It

Let's be clear, we don't recommend cheating at cards – it's anti-social and will lose you friends. However, many of the techniques used by card sharps have a place in the world of legitimate magic. They also improve your dexterity with the cards – and you can never have too much of that. The bottom deal is the hardest of the false deals included in this book and requires a good hand position to hold the cards correctly and perform the sleight unobtrusively.

Step 1

Here's the grip for the hand that's holding the deck. The corner nearest to you is at the base of your thumb and the corner furthest away rests, for now, on the first joint (not the knuckle) of your second finger.

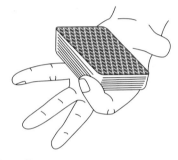

Step 2

Curl your first finger round the deck's front corner, then remove your other fingers, holding the deck between the base of your thumb and your first finger.

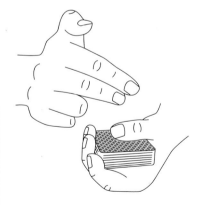

Step 3

Now let's look at the other hand because that finger position is crucial too. Hold it like this, with your first and second fingers out straight, held together, and your third and fourth finger bent into the palm as if you are making a fist.

Step 4

Okay, here we're looking at the bottom of the deck so you can see the finger positions when we bring both hands together to take a card from here. The second finger of our right hand slips between the first and second fingers of our left hand to get at those precious bottom cards.

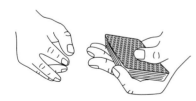

Step 5

Moving the right hand away, let's look again at your left hand's opening position as it holds the cards. Notice that the deck is held by the first finger and the ball of the thumb, which allows the other three fingers to point out straight.

Step 6

Bring your right hand in, mesh those fingers underneath (see Step 4) and then push the top card out sideways with your left thumb as if you were making a normal deal.

Step 7

Place your right thumb on the top card as if to take it, but instead, concentrate on pulling the bottom card out underneath.

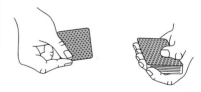

Step 8

The final movement of your right hand is like an upward slap to snap the card out from under the deck and onto the table. At the same time, draw the top card back with your left thumb, ready to deal again.

Skill
Pop-Out Card

Difficulty: 7

Objective
To make a card 'fly' out of the deck, seemingly at random.

How To Do It
A flourish to conclude any kind of find-the-card trick. Having forced the card to the bottom of the deck (see page 120) you then produce it with a fast snap.

Step 1
Having forced your chosen card to the bottom of the deck, you want to hold the pack lengthways, as deep into your hand as possible.

Step 2
We'll show it face forward so you can see the grip. Take your fingers and fold them around the edge of the deck as far as they'll go; this is a case where those with larger hands are at an advantage.

Step 3
Next, use your first three fingers to pivot the bottom card to your left while at the same time lifting it out slightly from the pack – you may find it useful to use your little finger to control this movement.

Step 4
Now use your other hand, palm up between the bottom card and the rest of the deck. Push forward to sandwich the card between the tips of the fingers of your left hand and your right.

Step 5
Continue pushing so the card bends and snaps forward into position, face up. Move the pack while you're doing this, keep the patter going and they'll never realize what's going on.

Skill
The Glide

Difficulty: **5**

Objective

To make the audience think the bottom card has changed since you last showed it to them.

How To Do It

This simple technique can be used in more complicated tricks, or even on its own, to fool the audience into thinking you've changed the bottom card on the deck. Success depends on how well you can perfect the grip and how smoothly you can perform the slide. Here we go.

Step 1

Hold the full deck in your hand with your thumb on one side and all four

fingers on the other. Get it deep into your palm because you'll need to get all the purchase you can with your second, third and further fingers. If you're using the glide as a stand-alone trick, show the bottom card to the audience.

Step 2

In order to show the technique, we'll keep the cards held up – in a trick, you'd have the pack face down. While you're talking to the audience, you want to use your second, third and fourth finger to slide the bottom card back toward you by about a finger's width.

Step 3

This allows you to reach under the deck and pull out the 'bottom card', which is actually now the one above it. With a little practice you can easily feel the new bottom card with your finger and thumb and reveal it to the audience to demonstrate that the card has changed.

Skill
Controlling a Card: Overhand Shuffle

Difficulty: 5

Objective

To control the position of a card in the deck while doing an Overhand Shuffle.

How To Do It

This is almost a trick rather than a skill, but being able to control the movement of a card within the pack is crucial to many tricks, so we've included it here. Essentially we're going to demonstrate how you can get a card to the top of the deck and keep it there, even while shuffling and even if it's been put into the middle of the deck.

Step 2

Drop one or two cards from the pile in your right hand on top of the pile in your left. Make sure these don't line up, that they're offset from the rest of the pile.

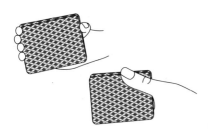

Step 1

We'll start with the easy one. Put a distinctive card on the top of the deck and then begin to do a standard Overhand Shuffle. Drop one half of the deck into your left hand, like so. Remember, the card we're interested in is on top of the pile in your left hand.

Step 3
Then, continue adding cards to the top of the new pile, but be sure to offset them first one way, and then the next. This will ensure that the initial offset is less obvious.

Step 4
Next, come round the back of the pile with your right hand – which is now empty – and push forward slightly. This will allow you to see where the first offset cards were dropped and thus where the original top card is – behind them.

Step 5
As you square up the deck, use your thumb to keep a gap where the original top card is on the side furthest away from the audience – shown here from above.

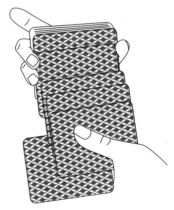

Step 6
Shuffle again, making sure that your thumb maintains the gap where the audience can't see it. Then, when there are only a few cards left to shuffle before you hit the gap, drop the last packet into your other hand and then drop the remaining cards – with the original card on top – onto the rest of the pack.

Skill
Riffle Force

Difficulty: 3

Objective
To move a card 'through' the deck from the top to somewhere in the middle.

How To Do It
Although this can be used as a simple mind-reading trick on its own, we're including it in the Skills section because, like all forces, it's useful in lots of different tricks. Performed with panache, it's impossible for an audience member to see how it's done. And as forces go, it's dead easy.

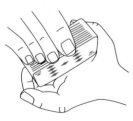

Step 1
You need to know what the top card is because this is the card you're going to force through the pack. No matter which card the audience thinks

they're choosing, it will always be this one! Hold the cards like so with your first three fingers and thumb on the top.

Step 2
Riffle through the cards and ask the audience to say stop at any time when they want to pick a card.

Step 3
You've got a ready-made gap in the pack and you're

holding the front edge of the cards firmly in your left hand anyway because it's controlling the riffle. All you have to do now is to turn the pack slightly, press down on the top card with your first three fingers, and then pull the rest of the pack out with your left hand.

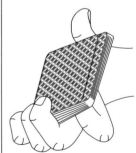

Step 4
This will slap the top card down onto the bottom half of the deck. Since you know what the top card is already, you can tell the audience the card that they've chosen.

Skill
Triple False Cut

Difficulty: 2

Objective
To keep a deck of cards in the same order while appearing to cut them thoroughly. Always useful when you need to control the order of the pack for one trick or another.

Step 1
To prove to yourself this works, take a standard deck of cards and sort it into suits, in running order – that way you'll be able to tell whether the cards keep their order or not. Then, start by holding the deck sideways on, landscape-style like this in two hands; the grip's not really important.

Step 2
Pull about a third of the deck out from the bottom with one hand like this and then bring it round and put it on top of the deck.

Step 3
As you do, use your thumb to keep a gap at the back that the audience can't see. We've turned the deck round to show you in this illustration.

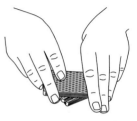

Step 4
Then, take another third off the bottom of the deck in exactly the same way and bring it round and put it on the top, but this time don't leave a gap.

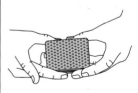

Step 5
Finally, pull out the rest of the cards – from the gap downward – bring them round and put them on top of the pack. This completes a thorough-looking triple cut without changing the order of the cards at all!

Skill
Hindu Shuffle Control

Difficulty: 4

Objective
To perform a realistic Hindu Shuffle that keeps a specific card where you want it.

How To Do It
Use this as part of any magic trick that requires you to find a card that, in reality, is on top of the deck.

Step 1
Make sure you know how to do a real Hindu Shuffle (see pages 92–3). Start with the card you want on top. Then, pull out around two thirds of the deck, but be sure to grip it with the first joint of your finger and thumb, rather than the tips. Once you've removed some cards with your other hand, let the first pile fall into the palm of the hand that was holding it. Your card is on the top of this pile.

Step 2
Place the rest of the pack on top of the pile in your palm, but angle it forward so the audience can't see you leave a gap between the top card on the bottom pile and the pack that you're adding to it.

Step 3
To the audience it should look as if

you've got three piles of cards – one in your palm, a big one in the middle that you're holding still, and a small one at the top that you're stripping off as the next part of the shuffle. In fact there are four; as you strip the second packet off the top ready to drop it into the palm of your hand, you're using that to conceal the fact that at the same time you've lifted part of the original packet (with the top card on it) with your other hand to form the central packet. From the front this looks like a single packet, but from the back you're using your little finger to maintain a gap, so you always know where the top card is. Our original top card is the first card under the gap being pinched between the right-hand thumb.

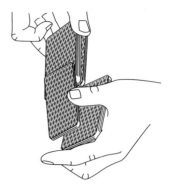

Step 5

Move your right hand forward again and pull some more cards off the top and let them fall into your other hand.

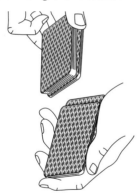

Step 4

Now carefully pull the middle section away with your right hand and let the other cards drop into the palm of your left hand.

Step 6

Keep stripping the cards from the top of your right hand until you reach the gap that marks where the original top card is. Make sure that you strip the cards above it, leaving it as the top card. Then drop it on the rest of the pile.

Skill
Card Clip

Difficulty: 3

Objective
To take a card from the deck without any of the audience seeing you do it.

How To Do It
Sometimes it's important to be able to take a card from the pack without anyone noticing, and the Card Clip is the easiest technique in this book. The only problem is making sure your hand position is correct and that you don't grab so much of the card that it can be seen between your fingers.

Step 1
Fan the deck and get someone to pick a card at random. Tell them to look at it. Riffle the deck and get them to tell you where to stop. When they say 'stop', cut the deck at that point and get them to put the card back. Just as you're preparing to put the rest of the pack on top of the chosen card, use your thumb to push it out to the side ever so slightly, as if you were about to deal it. Your other hand should give you enough cover so that the audience don't see.

Step 2
As you square the deck up, pinch the corner of the chosen card between the first joint nearest the knuckle of your third and little fingers.

Step 3
Ease the card out of the pack with as natural a movement as you can make. Talk to the audience to cover the move, and keep the hand straight as if you were going to shake someone's hand. From there you can palm it or drop it onto the top of the deck.

Skill
Palm a Card

Difficulty: 4

Objective
To take the top card without anyone seeing.

How To Do It
Along with having an ace up your sleeve, the notion of palming a card has been a mainstay of gambling movies for years. But how do you actually go about doing it? The answer is easy and quick to master. All you need is a big enough hand.

Step 1
The technique for palming a card is pretty simple. First, you need to jog the top card forward slightly by no more than a finger width. You can do this as part of a general movement of rearranging and squaring the deck.

Step 2
Then, you want to put your other hand over the top of the deck, obscuring it, and push down with the ends of your fingers onto the edge of the top card that's furthest away from you.

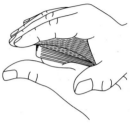

Step 3
This causes the other end of the card to flip up into the palm of your hand. By applying gentle pressure you can make a slightly 'C' shape with your hand – just enough to keep the card there when you lift the hand away.

Step 4
And here's what it looks like the other way up.

Skill

Palm a Card: Tenkai

Difficulty: 5

Objective

To palm a single card without the audience suspecting, and in a way that allows you to continue handling the cards.

How To Do It

This is a step up from the simple palm, but allows you to continue handling the cards with the tips of the fingers that are doing the palming.

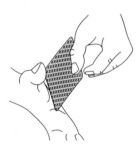

Step 1

Open one of your hands wide like this and find the rough centre line in the palm. This is where one edge of the card is going to sit, as shown here.

Step 2

Hold the other edge with your thumb. Practise moving your hand until you're happy with the grip.

Step 3

Some people prefer to bend the card slightly between palm and thumb. This helps those with smaller hands conceal the card, but it also allows everyone more leeway.

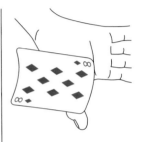

Step 4

Here's the grip shown face on so you can see where the card 'sits' in your hand.

Step 5

And here's the final hand position. Practise this one in front of a mirror to get your angles right. Although it's an excellent palm, it doesn't allow much leeway before the audience can see what you're up to.

Skill
Not-So-Fancy False Cut

Difficulty: 3

Objective
To cut the deck three times, but keep it in the same order.

How To Do It
This three-stage cut appears to shuffle the cards, but actually preserves their order.

Step 1
Hold the cards as for a pivot cut; pivot the top third with your first finger.

Step 2
Take the top third into the crook of your left thumb and, as you do, pivot out the next third with the first finger of your right hand.

Step 3
Holding the first third of the pack in your left hand, take the next third between your first finger and thumb. The first third should rest in the palm, while the second third is held by forefinger and thumb, resting on your outstretched fingers.

Step 4
Flip the second part of the deck so that it is vertical.

Step 5
Drop the last third onto the bottom of the vertical set.

Step 6
Lift both of those, flip the remaining cards into the vertical position, and drop the other cards onto the bottom.

Step 3

Step 4

Step 1

Step 5

Step 2

Step 6

Skill
Fancy False Cut

Difficulty: 5

Objective

To cut the deck three times, seemingly mixing the cards up while actually keeping them in the same order.

How To Do It

There's no real sleight of hand here; the deception arises when the cut is made at speed. Turning part of the deck over at the midpoint throws the audience and distracts them from the fact that the deck stays in order. You can also use it to keep specific cards on the top or bottom of the deck.

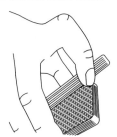

Step 1

Start by holding the deck of cards face down, with your thumb at the back on the short length and fingers at the front. Then, lift and separate about a third of the pack with your first finger, and then swing it out like so. (It's actually the beginning of the Pivot Cut from page 107).

Step 2

Bring your other hand in and slot the top third of the deck into the crook of your thumb so you can hold it there without using your other fingers.

Step 3

Next, let those cards drop into the palm of your hand, while with your other you pull and pivot off another third of the pack in the same way as you did in Step 1.

Step 4

With two thirds of the pack still split in your right hand, bring it over to your left hand and grasp the first third of the deck that's nestling in the palm of your left hand. Do not let go of the cards in your right hand.

Step 5

Instead, hold all three parts of the deck with your thumb at the back and your fingers like this: third finger on the bottom third, second finger on the middle third and first finger on the top third. Then swing out the top third into the crook of the thumb in your left hand with another pivot.

Step 6

Left hand first: You've got a third of the deck in the crook of your thumb. Put your first finger underneath the cards and grip them on top with your thumb and

second finger. Then lift your thumb out of the way and push with your first finger, opening your hand slightly, and start flipping the cards over so that they're face up. With your right hand, pivot the next section of the deck over toward your left hand.

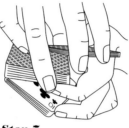

Step 7

You've now got the bottom third, face up, gripped between the first and second fingers of your left hand; the other cards are face down. The top third goes into the crook of your left thumb. The middle third is held with the right hand between the other two thirds.

Step 8

Left hand only: What we're going to do now is put the face-up part of the deck

onto the face-down part of the deck. Use your first finger to squeeze the bottom third and start to lift your thumb out of the way.

Step 9

Still left hand: As you squeeze with your first finger and lift your thumb, use your other fingers to flip the face-up part of the deck over and onto the face-down part of the deck in your palm.

Step 10

With the right hand, pop the top part of the deck onto the cards in the palm of your left hand. Despite the apparent complexity and thoroughness of the cut, the top card will be the same.

Skill
Super-Fancy False Cut

Difficulty: 8

Objective
To cut the deck a number of times, seemingly mixing the cards up while actually keeping the deck in exactly the same order.

How To Do It
This builds on the pivot cut, the Not-So-Fancy False Shuffle and the Fancy False Shuffle by introducing a bunch of unexpected twists and turns that make it impossible for the casual observer to realize that the cards are staying in exactly the same order.

Step 1
Open the deck into three parts like this. Your right thumb controls all the

cards from the back, the second finger lifts the top two thirds, the first finger then lifts the top third, and you can then let your left palm drop away and just hold the bottom third with the first finger.

Step 2
Just bring the third finger of your right hand down and use it to grip the bottom packet, thus freeing up your left hand for the next step.

Step 3
Bring the thumb of your left hand forward to push against the front of the middle packet and swing it out anticlockwise, using your right thumb, which is still at the back, as the pivot.

Step 4
Swing it all the way out and round and it'll just drop naturally into the palm of your left hand like so.

Step 5

Right hand only: Holding the top and bottom packets, rotate your wrist so that your fingers are on the bottom and your thumb is on the top.

Step 6

You then want to take the bottom packet with the thumb, first and second fingers of your left hand so it makes an 'L' shape with the packet that's already lying in your left palm.

Step 7

Left hand again: This is where you need some good stretch because you need to shift the packet in the palm of your hand up until the back of the cards rests against the base of your thumb. Use your two middle fingers to do this while the first and little finger keep the other packet steady against the top of your thumb.

Step 8

This is the hard bit! You then use the tips of the fingers of your left hand to rotate the packet they're holding anticlockwise

through 180 degrees so that the short edge that was at the back is now at the front.

Step 9

Once the rotation is complete, let the packet drop into the palm of your hand.

Step 10

Then drop the other packet in your left hand on top of it.

Skill
Super-Fancy False Cut (continued)

Step 11
Back with the right hand: Use your first finger to open the packet there as we did in Step 1.

Step 12
Use your left thumb to rotate the top packet in your right hand anticlockwise, pivoting against your right thumb. This is hard. Take it all the way to the back until the top packet is actually behind your right thumb.

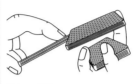

Step 13
Then rotate back to the front clockwise, passing underneath the top packet like so.

Step 14
Maintain the gap between the two packets in your right hand and then take the top one with your left thumb again. This time, pivot it anticlockwise and drop it onto the pack in your left hand using the same movement described in Steps 3 and 4.

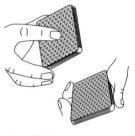

Step 15
Then drop the last packet onto the top of the deck in your left hand. The cards are in exactly the same order as they were when you started.

Skill
Thumb Throw

Difficulty: 3

Objective
To toss one or more cards without appearing to move your hand.

How To Do It
This is the sort of technique that you can use to improve your overall control of the pack. It's also a useful flourish to use at the end of a trick where you've brought a specific card to the top of the pack by devious means and want to reveal it with a bit of drama rather than just laying it on the table.

Step 1
Hold the deck parallel to your body, landscape-style, with the longer edges facing toward and away from you. The grip's the thing here, and is shown from above for clarity. You need to hold the card firmly between your first and fourth fingers, almost squeezing the pack together. Your second and third fingers are underneath the pack.

Step 2
You need to get your thumb as far into the near corner as you can without hurting yourself; the closer it gets to the corner, the more 'flick' you'll be able to achieve and the further the card will fly. Interestingly, more power will also give you more control over where the card ends up.

Step 3
Push hard onto the deck with the tip of your thumb and flick away from you in a kind of fast clockwise movement – at the same time, squeeze a little harder with your first and fourth fingers to make sure the rest of the pack stays put. To control the card even more, add a flick to the wrist as well – this will help guide the card. It's not an easy skill – most of the challenge is getting the grip right – but it's a neat technique and a very effective way of closing certain tricks.

Skill
Simple Card Throw

Difficulty: 4

Objective

To misdirect the audience into believing you've put down a certain card when you've put down another.

How To Do It

You can incorporate this technique into many of the tricks shown later, but here we'll just look at the mechanics of the technique. Essentially it's about holding two cards in your hand and convincing the audience that you've thrown down the one nearest to them, when in fact you're throwing down the one behind it.

Step 1

Take a couple of cards and make sure they're visually very different – say a 2 of spades and

a queen of hearts. Hold them one behind the other, like so, with the thumb at the top and two fingers at the bottom.

Step 2

Here's the same grip viewed from the front. Now what you're going to do is throw a card onto the table top. Of course, everyone expects it to be the card at the front, but actually it's just as easy to let go of the one at the back.

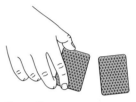

Step 3

Because of the speed of the throw, the audience's collective eye will simply assume you've thrown the first card, because logic dictates that's what you should do. It's a classic, simple piece of misdirection.

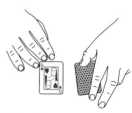

Step 4

In fact, when you turn the card over, you can see the cards have been switched.

Skill
Card Swing

Difficulty: 2

Objective

To throw the deck onto the floor or against a wall while retaining two chosen cards in your hand.

How To Do It

This is a very simple technique that many people can do the very first time they try it. It allows you to throw a full deck of cards while retaining the top and bottom cards in your hand to show to the audience after the throw. It combines a nice bit of flash – boy, those cards go everywhere – and uses science rather than skill.

Step 1

Use one of the other techniques mentioned elsewhere to manoeuvre

your chosen cards to the top and bottom of the deck – there are any number of false shuffles you can use. Alternatively, just set it up beforehand.

Step 2

There's no fancy grip. Just hold the deck toward the bottom with your thumb on the top and first three fingers on the bottom. Give the deck a bit of a squeeze and then flick your wrist to the right…

Step 3

…and then to the left. Swing the pack to build up some anticipation, chatting to the audience all the while.

Step 4

Stop squeezing the deck at the end of a swing. The friction from your thumb and fingers will help the top and bottom cards stick, while the others fly all over the place. As they go, the top and bottom cards snap together in your hand. Turn them over and show the audience.

Skill
Pirouette Flourish

Difficulty: 6

Objective
To take a single card from the deck and spin it round on the top of one finger.

How To Do It
This is a great flourish for any trick. Tricky at first, once you can pull this off, the Pirouette Flourish becomes a graceful movement.

Step 1
The grip is the key. Take a single card and hold it face up between your thumb on the top and your second finger on the bottom. Some people find it easier to use a card like the ace that has a 'pip' in the centre to help them work out where to put their thumb.

Step 2
Then, put your first finger next to your second finger on the back of the card as shown here.

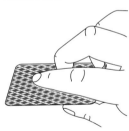

Step 3
Next, keep the card turned over so you can see the back, and then push your first finger forward so it lays flat on the back of the card. This will have the natural effect of rotating the card clockwise.

Step 4
Now pull your first finger back quickly and the card will spin back in the opposite direction. Try it again, but this time don't grip the card so tightly with your thumb and second finger. Practise until you can spin the card in a complete circle once.

Step 5
When you can do that, you need to practise removing your thumb and first finger, leaving the card balancing on your second finger so it can spin.

Skill
Rising Card

Difficulty: 4

Objective

To produce your chosen card from the top of the deck by making it appear to rise up of its own accord.

How To Do It

This simple technique can be used at the end of a trick after you've positioned the chosen card on top of the deck. It's just an alternative way of displaying the card and can be tacked onto any trick that ends by revealing the top card.

Step 1

Perform the trick – whatever it is – so that the chosen card ends up on the top of the pack. Then, to make it nice and easy,

do a little finger lift to separate the top card from the rest of the deck.

Step 2

Turn the cards to face the audience and put the first finger of your other hand on the top like this. At the same time, use the little finger of the same hand to feel for the bottom of the top card.

Step 3

Slowly lift the card up the pack with your little finger.

Step 4

From the front it looks as if the card is rising of its own accord.

Skill
Basic Ribbon Spread

Difficulty: 3

Objective

To spread the cards out across the table in front of you.

How To Do It

This can be used with the cards face down as a simple flourish before beginning a trick, or with the cards face up to demonstrate that it's a normal, full deck. Either way, it looks great and can be extended easily to flip the cards over in different ways, as we'll see a bit later on. For now though, let's look at the Basic Ribbon Spread.

Step 1

You can't do this on a smooth surface like a wood or laminate table;

you need some cloth like felt. You can even use a plain cotton t-shirt if it's spread out on a flat surface. If you don't have a surface that the cards can 'grip', you can't do a ribbon spread. Hold the pack like this with two fingers on the front short edge, first finger on the long side, and thumb at the back.

Step 2

What you're going to do is use your first finger to control the cards as you spread the deck across the table. This takes a bit of practice, but before long you'll be able to feel the way to raise your first finger slightly to release cards gradually as your hand moves from left to right.

Step 3

Next, put the pack face down on the table and then, with a smooth motion, move your hand from left to right, releasing cards with your first finger as you go.

Step 4

Finding it harder than you expected? Try adjusting your grip slightly so that you use two fingers instead of just one. Some people find this helps them to control the cards more effectively.

Skill

Ribbon Spread, Turnover and Scoop

Difficulty: 4

Objective

Having fanned the cards out across the table in front of you, you turn them over and then scoop them up with your other hand.

How To Do It

This follows on from the previous page and adds a couple of simple moves that look great at the beginning of a trick. It allows you to fan the cards out, flip them over to show it's a full deck, and then gather them up in your other hand ready to go.

Step 1

Do the ribbon fan as described on the previous page. Then, put the fingers of your left hand under the card at the end of the ribbon on that side.

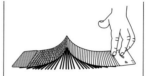

Step 2

Then, just lift the end card up with a confident, smooth motion, and let the rest of the cards do the work. When you get it right, their momentum just keeps the cards turning over one by one, like falling dominoes.

Step 3

Have your right hand ready and, as the end cards start to turn, just slip it under them, palm up so the last cards fall into it. Then you can bring your right hand in to meet your left hand, scooping up the cards as you go.

Step 4

Alternatively, when the cards land in your right hand, you can use it to flip them all back in the opposite direction. This gives you complete control over whether the cards end up face up or face down on the table.

Skill
Ribbon Spread Turnover Control

Difficulty: 5

Objective
Having fanned the cards out across the table in front of you, you turn them over using first your finger and then another playing card.

How To Do It
This adds a nice extra flourish to the Basic Ribbon Spread and Turnover by allowing you to control the speed and direction of the turn, even stopping it midway or going in both directions. Once you've mastered the basic spread, this is dead easy to do.

Step 1
Do the Basic Ribbon Spread exactly as before (see page 140) and then, once you've lifted the end card to begin the turnover, take the finger of your other hand and place it on the top edge of the cards.

Step 2
You can now use your finger to control the speed and direction of the turnover, stopping in the middle if you like and then going back the other way. It looks difficult but is actually very easy.

Step 3
You can also use the end card itself to control the turnover. Lift the end card as usual, take it out with your right hand, and turn it to face the audience.

Step 4
Now you can use the edge of the card to roll the turnover back and forth from left to right in front of you. It looks great and, again, is very easy.

Step 1

Step 2

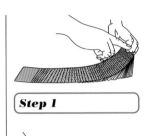

Step 3

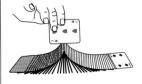

Step 4

Skill
Double Ribbon Spread Turnover Control

Difficulty: **6**

Objective

Having fanned the cards out across the table in front of you, use the edges of two cards to make the halves of the pack turn over back and forth, independently of each other.

How To Do It

This is the final piece of work we'll be doing with the Ribbon Spread Turnover Control, and is the best visual effect yet. The two cards facing the audience add some visual interest and the way the cards roll back and forth across the table makes this a very effective flourish that is relatively easy to master. Once you've got the Basic Ribbon Spread down (see page 140), the rest is straightforward.

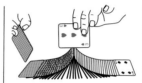

Step 1

Do the Basic Ribbon Spread and then practise turning it over using the edge of a single card (see opposite). Bring the card into the middle of the deck and then, with your other hand, take a card from the other end of the pack.

Step 2

Bring the second card in behind the first and then use it to split the pack at the centre point. This takes a bit of dexterity but you'll soon get the hang of

it. You should now be able to control one half of the deck with either hand.

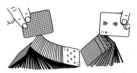

Step 3

Move the cards back and forth, join them in the middle again, separate them again and so on until you're finished. Remember that the deck will inevitably slip after a turn or two, so you will lose control of the cards eventually.

Skill
Final Card Flourish

Difficulty: 4

Objective
To produce a single card at the end of a trick with a bit of pizzazz.

How To Do It
Although this looks complex, it's actually relatively simple. It requires you to hold a break between two packets of cards in your left hand, but this is straightforward; as with most flourishes, it's the twists and turns of the hands and cards that provide the entertainment, rather than any really fancy finger movements.

Step 1
Start with a pivot cut (see page 107). Hold the deck in your right hand, thumb

at the back, first three fingers at the front and then lift up the top half of the deck with your first finger and swing it left.

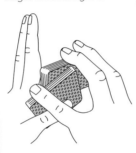

Step 2
Bring your left hand in and slot the top packet into the crook of your thumb like this.

Step 3
Let the packet drop into the palm of your left hand, then use the second two

fingers of your right hand to divide the remaining cards into two.

Step 4
Rotate your right hand forward and then bring your left hand to take the bottom part of the packet.

Step 5
Notice that the new packet is placed halfway up the bottom packet in the left hand.

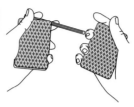
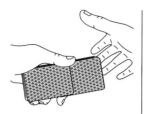

Step 6
Place the final packet in your right hand on top of the others in your left hand so the top and bottom packets line up and the middle one sticks out. This helps you feel the break in the deck and maintain it.

Step 7
Use your right hand to pull the middle packet out while still keeping the break with your left hand.

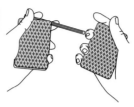

Step 8
Notice the position of the first and second fingers of the left hand. This allows you to flip the top packet up – remember you've still kept the break there – like so.

Step 9
Pass the packet over to your right hand like this.

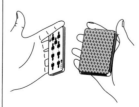

Step 10
Lay the packet down on top of the one already in your right hand. Then, with your left, let the

packet pivot away from the palm of your hand.

Step 11
When the packet in your left hand is laying flat on your last three fingers, roll the packet in your right hand over and on top of it.

Step 12
Then use your right hand to flip the deck over again into the palm of your left hand. As you do, pull out the top card – actually on the bottom of the deck as we look at it – with your right hand. This is the original top card.

Skill
Prepping a Deck NO.1

Difficulty: **2**

Objective

To show a deck to the audience that looks as though it's been thoroughly shuffled but which is, in fact, ordered in a very specific way. This particular setup is called the Si Stebbins deck, after its creator.

How To Do It

Most people think it's easy to spot a deck that's been tampered with. They're wrong! We're going to explain how to prep a deck that can be used for lots of different tricks and that you can show to the average audience with complete confidence.

Step 1

Here's the deck. We've shuffled it and then fanned it out so you can see the cards. Don't forget the audience will only get a quick glance, while you have the chance to study it. Looks normal, right?

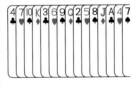

Step 2

Look more closely and you'll see that in fact, the cards are in strict order. Count the face cards like this: a jack is 11, a queen is 12 and a king is 13; the ace is one. Starting with the 4 of clubs, choose subsequent cards by adding three. So, the sequence goes 4, 7, 10, king (13) and then continues with 3, 6, 9 and queen (12).

Step 3

There's one more thing to notice with this particular deck setup. The suits run in sequence as well – it's called the CHaSeD order and runs clubs, hearts, spades and diamonds. What this means is you can start with a deck, do a few false shuffles to preserve the order, fan it out, show the audience, yet have all the cards in a specific order that allows you to do tricks. We'll show you a good one on page 166.

Skill
Prepping a Deck NO.2

Difficulty: **2**

Objective

To set a deck up so that a member of the audience, following your instructions, can divide the pack perfectly into black suits and red suits.

How To Do It

This is a simple bit of preparation that allows you to start dividing the deck into black and red suits and then hand it over to a member of the audience to finish up. We'll show you how to do the trick on page 178 but for now, here's the setup.

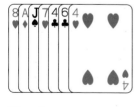

Step 1

Take seven cards out of the pack. Make them a mix of red and black, but make sure you can remember the sequence. To make the trick work

you need two red, one black, one red, two black and one red. Choose any denomination of card you like, but keep that sequence.

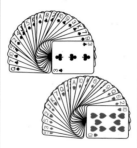

Step 2

That leaves you with 22 red cards and 23 black cards. Arrange them together as shown here. Again, the sequence of the cards isn't important; what matters is that all the red cards are together and all the black cards are together.

Step 3

Finally, arrange the deck as shown here. The sequence of red and black cards go on the top. Follow that by all the red cards and then finish with all the black cards. This simple setup allows you to do the great Black and Red Decks trick on page 178.

Skill
Prepping a Deck NO. 3

Difficulty: 2

Objective

To set a deck up with a hidden sequence that only you're aware of and that can be used in various tricks. This one's usually called 'eight kings'.

How To Do It

Here's another simple deck preparation that produces a card sequence that's hard for an audience to spot, but is easy for you to remember.

Step 1

We're going to divide the deck into four groups of 13 cards, all arranged using the same technique. First, the suits. These go in CHaSeD order (see page 146), which means that they must always follow the clubs, hearts, spades, diamonds sequence.

Step 2

In addition to suit order, the cards are arranged in a specific order. To help you remember this, there's a little mnemonic that goes 'eight kings threaten to save 95 ladies for one sick knave'. Translated, that means eight (8 of clubs) kings (king of hearts) threa… (3 of spades) …ten (10 of diamonds) to (2 of clubs) save (7 of hearts) ninety (9 of spades) five (5 of diamonds) ladies (queen of clubs) for (4 of hearts) one (ace of spades) sick (6 of diamonds) knave (jack of clubs).

Step 3

Arrange the rest of the cards in the same order. This takes a while to get your head round, but so long as you follow the same number sequence and the same suit sequence, you'll be fine. So, for the next lot of 13 cards, start with the 8 of hearts, because hearts follows clubs in suit sequence and 8 is the beginning of the mnemonic.

Skill
Behind-the-Hand Grip

Difficulty: 6

Objective
To hide a card behind your hand where no one can see it.

How To Do It
This technique can be used in many different sleight-of-hand tricks. It's extremely versatile and, though a little awkward at first, will quickly become second nature. There's no stretch, you don't need hand strength or big hands, just practice.

Step 1
Start with a single card, held like so – with the thumb at the front corner and the first finger on the back. Notice the two middle fingers are folded into the palm.

Step 2
Bring your little finger round to the corner as shown and then bring your first finger round in the same way. When you can grip the card with your first and last fingers, you can let go with your thumb.

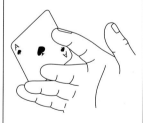

Step 3
Now, straighten your two middle fingers while still gripping the cards with your first and last fingers. This movement takes the card behind your hand.

Step 4
With all four fingers fully extended, it looks as though the card has disappeared. In fact, it's being held behind the hand with two corners gripped between the first and second and the third and fourth fingers.

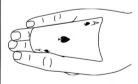

Step 5
Here's the view from behind the hand.

Skill
One-Handed Fan

Difficulty: 5

Objective
To spread the cards into an attractive fan shape with one hand.

How To Do It
This doesn't really do anything except look nice. It can be used to help an audience member pick a card and it will always make you look good, assuming you pull it off.

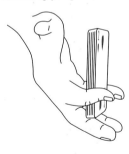

Step 1
Start by using half the deck. Once you've got the basics, you can work up to a full deck. Hold the cards like this – two middle fingers at the bottom, first and little finger either side, gripping the deck. You shouldn't need to use your thumb at all. This is shown sideways on.

Step 2
Bring your thumb down to the bottom left of the deck. As you do, bring your first and little fingers round to the front.

Step 3
Staying behind the deck, push your thumb to the right to start fanning the cards in that direction.

Step 4
From the front, you push your fingers to the left (in the opposite direction to your thumb) to fan the cards. The movement is a little like rubbing thumb and fingers together to indicate money.

Step 5
And here's the finished fan. Note the position of the fingers at the front.

Skill
Pressure Fan

Difficulty: **7**

Objective
To spread the cards into a large, attractive fan shape using two hands.

How To Do It
The Pressure Fan is a neat way to reassure an audience that you're working with an ordinary deck. It can also be used with the cards face down when offering them to a member of the audience to pick from. It's a little tricky to master but looks great when you've got the knack. If you find it too tough, try practicing it with half a deck to start.

Step 2
Take the cards in your other hand and hold them with two fingers at the front and your thumb at the back toward the outside edge and then squeeze the cards to put a slight curve in them.

Step 3
Face the cards forward and then position your other hand like so with the first finger pointing down toward the corner and the deck pinched between it

and the fleshy part of your thumb.

Step 4
Bend the cards slightly and then start to rotate your left hand as far round as it will go.

Step 5
Only then should you move your right hand in the opposite direction to complete the fan. It's tough, but with practice it looks fantastic.

Step 1
You want to start with the deck face down in your palm and slide the cards away from your thumb slightly to create a slope.

Skill
Ultra Fan

Difficulty: **6**

Objective

To spread the cards into an attractive pseudo-3D fan shape with two hands.

How To Do It

This requires less hand strength than the more difficult Pressure Fan, but there's still quite a lot of dexterity involved so you'll need to practise.

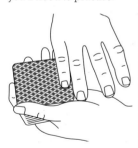

Step 1

Hold the deck in your left hand as if you were about to deal the cards. Then take your other hand and place your third and little finger along the bottom the deck as shown here. Grip the bottom of the deck with the thumb on the same hand.

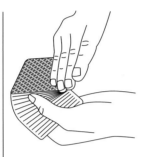

Step 2

Use your left hand underneath the deck to fan the cards anti-clockwise.

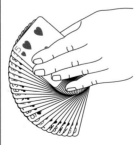

Step 3

When you reach the halfway mark, turn your right hand over so the cards are face up.

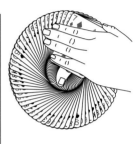

Step 4

As you sweep the fan round and continue to rotate your other hand so the cards are facing up, you need to drop your right thumb from its original position on top of the last card so it's underneath it. Then you can continue to sweep the cards over the thumb.

Step 5

And this is the finished fan. Looking good.

Skill
Tower of Cards

Difficulty: 7

Objective
To make a structure of playing cards that's at least three stories high.

How To Do It
This is about getting you comfortable with handling cards: how to hold them delicately but with control, and how to position them relative to each other. It'll also teach you patience, we promise you that!

Step 1
Use a surface that the cards can grip and a deck of cards that hasn't been beaten up too much. Place the first two cards a little away from each other and then lean them in until they support each other.

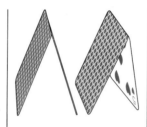

Step 2
After the first two have fallen over a few times they'll eventually stand up. Put the next two card beside them, leaving a small gap in between. You can guarantee that when the cards fall, they'll fall into each other and not the other way.

Step 3
Lay a fifth card delicately on top of the other two

like so. Make sure it sticks out a bit at either end to aid stability.

Step 4
Add another story to your building by gently placing two more cards on top. Try and get the bottom edges to line up roughly with a point midway down the back of the two slanting cards that make up the ground floor. Now go back to the bottom layer and add another pair of cards. Then you can add a second pair to the first floor and then put a third on top of those.

Section 3

Tricks

Trick
Bottoms Up

Difficulty: 3

Objective
To show the audience the bottom card and then change it for another right in front of them.

How To Do It
To prepare for this trick, all you need to do is have a couple of very different cards on the bottom of the deck – say the 2 of spades and the king of diamonds.

Step 1
Hold the deck as in the illustration above. It needs to be a nice snug grip so that you can support the cards with your thumb and get some really good pressure on them with your second, third and fourth fingers. Show the bottom card to the audience.

Step 2
Get the audience to tell you what the card is and then tell them you're going to change it. As you're talking to them, hold the deck face down and then use your three fingers to slide the bottom card down a bit so you can get at the card above it. We're showing you face on so you can see the move.

Step 3
Once you've pulled the bottom card back with your fingers, you can reach in and take the second-from-bottom card and show it to the audience. It takes a bit of time to get the grip and the pressure on the cards right, but you'll soon get the hang of it – in fact, by holding the cards face down (we've tilted the pack so you can see what's going on) you'll find that gravity makes it a bit easier.

Trick
Easy Slide NO.1

Difficulty: 2

Objective
To change one card into another right in front of the audience with no table involved.

How To Do It
This is the easiest card switch in the book and depends only on being able to do a 'double lift' (lifting two cards off the deck while pretending to lift only one) to work properly.

Step 1
Prepare the deck by choosing three top cards to go face up – choose something like the jack of hearts, the queen of clubs and the king of hearts. If you need to, prepare the double lift by easing the

corner nearest your little finger up off the deck, and then hold the deck face up with the short side facing the audience.

Step 2
Lift the back of the top card – actually the top two cards, courtesy of the double lift you've done – and slide it backward off the top of the pack to reveal the card underneath. Be very careful to keep the top two cards together so the audience doesn't suspect what's going on.

Step 3
Slide the cards forward again and give the audience some chat. As you do, use your thumb to drop the hidden card onto the deck so that now you're really only holding the top card. Pull it back to reveal the new card that the audience hasn't seen before. With practice you'll be able to drop and pick up the hidden card at will. Choose something like the cards suggested here and you can punctuate the trick with patter like: 'Where's the queen?' 'There she is.' 'Where's the queen?' 'There she is.'

Trick
Easy Slide NO.2

Difficulty: 3

Objective
To change one card into another right in front of the audience with no table involved.

How To Do It
This is a nice easy switch trick that requires little skill. The only prerequisite is that you have hands big enough to conceal the card properly. The idea here is that you're going to swap the face-up card on top of the deck with the card underneath it by using a simple slide.

Step 1
Choose two cards to go face up on top of the deck that are different: a face and a plain card, a red and black suit.

Step 2
Square the deck up and then hold it in one hand, with the short edge facing the audience. Then slide the top card toward them with the tips of the fingers of your other hand.

Step 3
Next, move your hand forward so it covers the top card almost completely and then use the heel of the same hand to push down on the card underneath. We've lifted the hand up so you can see what's going on.

Step 4
Pull back your hand, continuing to push down with the heel of it. As you do, you'll pull out the card underneath until the end flips out from under the top card. All this happens in the palm of your hand, hidden from the audience. Again, we've lifted out the hand so you can see.

Patter
When you're doing close magic (sometimes called table magic) like this, it's important to get some good patter going. This distracts the audience from looking too closely at what your hands are doing.

If you can do it, find a few good one-liners from the Internet – people are even more easily distracted if they're laughing.

Step 5

Push your hand forward again, bringing the new top card with it. As your hand covers the old top card, so it's also covered by the new top card, hidden beneath the palm of your hand and unseen by your audience. Use your fingers to square up the end of the pack nearest the audience and then take your hand away to reveal the new top card. Voila – it's changed.

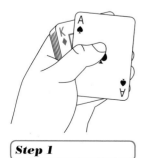

Step 1

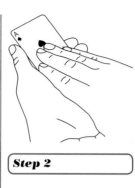

Step 2

Step 3

Step 4

Step 5

Trick
If Six Were Nine

Difficulty: 2

Objective
The audience hides a black 6 and a black 9 in the deck. Then you find it in one move.

How To Do It
This uses the Card Swing from page 137, so take a look at that first. It uses a tiny sleight of hand and a bit of misdirection – and very little skill!

Step 1
Before the audience arrives, find the 6 of clubs, the 6 of spades, the 9 of clubs and the 9 of spades. Put the 6 of clubs on the bottom and the following cards on the top in order: 9 of spades, then the 6 of spades, then the 9 of clubs.

Step 2
Deal someone the two cards from the top – the 9 of clubs and the 6 of spades. Get them to look at the cards and ask them to remember them.

Step 3
Get them to put the cards back somewhere in the middle of the pack. Don't let them put them on the top or the bottom.

Step 4
Now scratch your head, say how hard this trick is… anything to take their mind off their cards. Then, use the throw technique from page 137 to hurl the deck to the floor.

Step 5
You'll now hold the top and bottom cards. If you've done your job, people will see a black 6 and 9 – and won't realize they're not the right suits.

Trick
Float a Card NO.1

Difficulty: 2

Objective
To take an ordinary playing card and make it float over your open palms.

How To Do It
This is a great little trick which needs no setup and no special equipment. It also relies on audience over-thinking – because despite the fact that it's pretty obvious what's going on, they'll often assume something more intricate is happening, or that you're using a prop, or have a little device hidden behind your hands. Make a crack about not using sticky tape or a bent matchstick or anything else. You have nothing to declare but the power of your own mind.

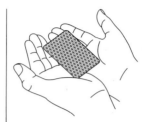

Step 1
Lay a playing card flat on the palms of your hands so that you can see the three longer fingers of each hand. It's important these remain in sight at all times. Give the audience some preparatory chat.

Step 2
Cup the card ever so slightly to give yourself a bit of room underneath it. Then, using the stronger of your two little fingers, simply bend it in toward

your palm, getting it as close to the centre of the card as possible. Then 'levitate' the card.

Step 3
Here's the view from the side of the hand where you can clearly see the card is being lifted by the little finger. It doesn't matter if it wobbles around (levitating anything is hard work), and at the end you can give a little sigh of relief and let the card drop back into your hands. Then show the audience there's nothing behind either hand or under the card.

Trick
Aces High

Difficulty: 2

Objective

To tell the audience where the four aces are while appearing to let them cut and deal the deck randomly.

How To Do It

Find the four aces and then put them on top of the deck. It's another neat, simple trick that audiences will enjoy especially because after the setup you don't touch the cards at all.

Step 1

Extract all four aces and put them on top of the deck before the trick starts. Hand the deck to a member of the audience and get them to put it on the table. Then, tell them to cut the deck once and then cut the two resulting decks once each, so they end up with fours piles of cards of a similar size. As we look at it, the four aces are on top of the pile at the right.

Step 2

Get them to pick up the left-hand pile, count three cards off the top and put them to the bottom of the pile. Then, they should deal one card on top of each of the remaining three piles.

Step 3

Next, get them to pick up the pile next to the first pile and do the same. Take three cards from the top, put them to the bottom and then deal out one card to each of the other piles. Repeat for the remaining two piles of cards. Here we've finished and are putting the final pack down.

Step 4

Tell them that thanks to their efforts you now know where all the aces are. And to make things easier, you've made them move to the top of each pile. Turn the top card of each one over to reveal the aces one after the other.

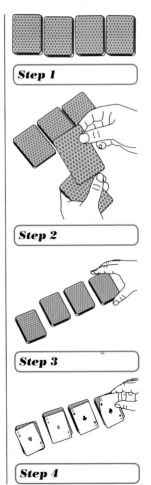

Step 1

Step 2

Step 3

Step 4

Trick
Float a Card NO.2

Difficulty: 2

Objective

To take an ordinary playing card and make it float over the palm of one hand.

How To Do It

This is a variation of Float a Card NO.1, on page 161, that adds a prop – in this case another playing card – and uses a very simple deception to make the audience believe that the card is floating over the top of your open palm. There's no preparation and, as before, no strings, tape or anything else attached.

Step 1

Pick a single card from the deck. You can do this

however you like because the identity of the card isn't important. Then, hold your right hand out, palm up like this. Then, as you place the chosen card face down on it, move your first finger slightly to the left and over the middle finger.

Step 2

Place the card gently on the palm of your hand – actually, you're placing it on your first finger – covering the palm up hand with the other hand as you do it.

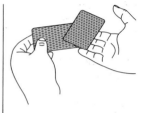

Step 3

Balancing the card on your first finger looks OK, but the impressive part comes next – just take another card from the deck and pass it under the 'floating' card like so. If you move the second card in an ellipse round the 'floating' card it will deceive the audience into thinking that the card passes completely underneath, instead of round the side of the first finger.

Trick
Simple Card Count

Difficulty: 1

Objective
To make a spectator pick your chosen card.

How To Do It
This simple trick works every time and is easily mastered. There's minimal setup, though you will need to prime the deck, and anyone can learn how to do it in a few moments. Like many of the easiest card tricks, it's based on simple mathematics. As a result, it is best performed at speed before the audience has a chance to work it out. Here's how it goes:

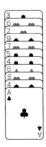

Step 1
Pick a memorable card like the ace of clubs or queen of hearts and then make sure it's the tenth card in the pack. Do this beforehand so the audience doesn't suspect. Tell the audience you're going to make them pick this card.

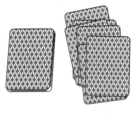

Step 2
Ask one of the audience to pick a number between ten and 20. Make it clear that they must choose between ten and 20, and can't pick either of those numbers. Let's say, for example, that someone chooses 16. Now, simply deal off 16 cards from the deck face down.

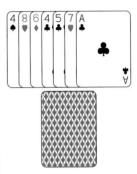

Step 3
Put the rest of the deck to one side and pick up the cards you just dealt, still holding them face down. Tell the audience that the chosen card – in this example, the ace of spades – is in that pile and then sift through them. In your head add the two numbers that go together to make up the number the spectator chose in Step 2 – in this example it's 16, or 1 + 6 which equals 7 (if it had been 19 it would equal 10). In this example, whichever card you chose in Step 1 will be the seventh card you deal out.

Trick
Devoted Sisters

Difficulty: 2

Objective
To have an audience member randomly place two black queens in the deck, which you can then use to find the two red queens.

How To Do It
This requires no sleight of hand and the simplest of setups. It's a good beginner's trick because its simplicity confers confidence.

Step 1
Before the audience arrives, take all four queens from the deck. Put one red queen on the top and the other red queen on the bottom of the deck. Now you're ready to begin. Give one of the audience the remaining two black queens.

Step 2
Start dealing from the pack face down. Ask the audience to stop you when they like. When they do, get them to put one of the black queens down on your pile, face up.

Step 3
When they've done that, put the rest of the pack down on top of the cards. Then start laying cards face down again until the audience tells you to stop. Then, they can put their remaining black queen down face up. Finish off by putting the rest of the deck on top of it. We've pulled the two black queens out slightly to illustrate.

Step 4
Cut the deck once, completely. Then tell the audience that the black queens are such devoted sisters that they've found the red queens on their own. Find the first upturned black queen – the card before it will be a red queen – and then do the same with the second. We've turned the red queens over already.

Trick
Pick Any Card

Difficulty: 2

Objective
To use a deck setup using the Si Stebbins order to predict the card that one of the audience chooses.

How To Do It
This simple trick relies on having the deck set up as described on page 146. Because the sequence appears random, you can even show people the deck face up first, in order to convince them the cards have been shuffled.

Step 1
Fan the cards out, face up to show that they've been shuffled. If you need to convince the audience further, use one of the false shuffles from earlier.

Step 2
Next, get a member of the audience to tap the back of any card in the pack.

Step 3
When they take it, put the pile that was on top of their chosen card underneath the other pile. Then tell them to look at their card. As they do, sneak a quick look at the bottom card of the pile.

Step 4
Because of the way the deck is ordered, it's now easy to tell them that their card is the 5 of spades. How? Because we know that the card before the one they chose is the 2 of hearts. Spades come after hearts in the Si Stebbins suit sequence, and the next card is always three more than the one before it.

Trick
Pile of Ten

Difficulty: 1

Objective
To present the audience with two piles of cards and then predict which pile they'll pick up.

How To Do It
This needs to be prepared beforehand, perhaps using a second deck that you can put to one side while you do some other tricks with another pack. Then you need to get a piece of paper and pencil.

Step 1
Before the audience arrives, prepare two piles of cards. Take out the four 10s to make one pile. For the other, use any ten cards. Place them face down on the table (we've shown them face up so you can see).

Step 2
Pick a member of the audience and look them in the eye for a moment or two. Then thank them. Next, without letting anyone see, take the pencil and paper and write 'I predict you will pick the pile of ten.' Fold the paper up and give it to them to put in their pocket.

Step 3
Get them to think hard and then ask them to turn one of the piles over. Then tell them to unfold the piece of paper in their pocket. No matter which pile they choose, you can say you've guessed correctly. If they pick the four 10s, turn over the other cards to show they're all different. If they pick the pile of ten cards, spread the other cards face down to show that there are only four of them.

Trick
Poker Trick

Difficulty: 2

Objective
To deal six people a full house in poker. And then to beat them with your hand, every time.

How To Do It
This uses the simplest of deck setups – arrange each suit starting with the ace low to king high; then put the four piles on top of each other. This ensures that the trick will work every time, even if you allow someone else to cut the deck. There's almost no counting involved, no sleight of hand, and you even show the audience that you're cheating on two occasions before throwing them off the scent by discarding your cards and starting again. It's a brilliantly simple trick for beginners.

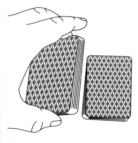

Step 1
Place the deck face down on the table. Tell the audience you're going to play them at poker. Get someone to cut the pack in half once. This should be a proper cut, taking half the pack off and putting beside, then taking the rest and putting it on top. Then get another person to cut the pack again.

Step 2
Deal out one card each to the six imaginary players

and then deal one for yourself.

Step 3
Do the same, but this time when you deal your own card, take it from the bottom. Do this deliberately, tell the audience what you're doing, and do it with a smile on your face.

Step 4
Deal another set of cards all from the top. Then deal a fourth set from the top for all the other players and from the bottom for yourself. Again, make no attempt to hide what you're doing. At the end of

this step everyone should have four cards each.

Step 5

Okay, now explain to the audience that you've had a change of heart. That it isn't fair you should be able to take cards from the bottom when you feel like it. Tell them you're going to throw your four cards away and put them to one side. Then, deal a final card to each player so they have five cards each, ready to play a hand of poker. Deal yourself five cards, from the top, one after the other.

Step 6

Tell the first player that you think they've got a good hand and get them

to turn it over. They'll have a full house.

Step 7

Get the other players to turn their hands over one after the other. Everyone will have a full house.

Step 8

Tell them you think they've all done really well to get such good hands, but that you're afraid it's not going to be enough. Then turn your hand over. You'll have a straight flush, which, sadly for everyone else, beats any number of full houses.

Cheating at Poker

It's almost expected, really, that everyone at some point has a go at cheating at poker. Of course, you should never do this in someone else's house, and never, ever do it in a gaming house of any description; but it's fun to have a go in the comfort and safety of your own home.

Aside from such staples as second card and bottom dealing, people have tried many ways to cheat at poker, palming chips while looking after the bank, marking cards and making false shuffles or cuts.

Card counting itself doesn't count as cheating, unless you get too good at it – and even though it's not against the law, casinos routinely ban players who are highly skilled counters.

Trick
Homing Card

Difficulty: 2

Objective
To make a card disappear from the deck and then teleport back to an empty packet.

How To Do It
This beautifully simple trick requires the slightest of setups – as you remove the deck of cards from the packet, you leave one in there and sneak a quick look so you know what it is. As it involves the packet, this is a good trick to start off a sequence or small show with.

Step 1
Make sure you know what the top card in the packet is before you start the trick. Then, open the packet with the flap facing the audience. This allows you to disguise the fact that as you're removing the cards, you're using your thumb to hold the top one back. Just be careful that it doesn't rattle around when put the supposedly empty packet back down on the table.

Step 2
Fan the cards out face down and get the audience to choose five cards at random. Lay them face down on the table. Then – and here's a switch – lift the cards one at a time and tell them what each card is (but don't show them). Get them to write each one down as you do. All you need to do is to replace the name of one of the cards with the name of the card in the packet (here we're replacing the king of spades with the ace of hearts). Because the audience don't see the cards, they won't suspect anything is wrong.

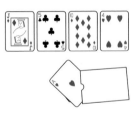

Step 3
Tell them to replace the cards in the pack, shuffle it, cut it, do what they like. Then get them to turn it over and find the five cards. One of them will be missing, because in fact it never left the packet. Tell them it must be a 'homing' card before producing it from the packet.

Trick
Throw Vanish

Difficulty: 7

Objective
To make a card disappear into thin air whilst flipping it between two fingers.

How To Do It
For this, you need to know how to do the Throw Deal on page 112 and the Tenkai variation of palming a card on page 128. There's no real point in attempting the trick until you've learned the techniques behind it. So, off you go and we'll see you back here in a minute.

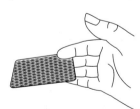

Step 1
Now you've mastered those skills, hold the card between your first and second finger as shown here. It needs to be held lightly. Then, keep your fingers straight and swing your wrist forward and

backward as if getting ready to throw the card.

Step 2
After a few swings, you want to bend your first two fingers in as if making a fist so that the card tucks into the middle of your palm and underneath the ball of your thumb.

Step 3
Hook your thumb over the top of the card – it doesn't matter if it bends a bit, as this will help to conceal

it more effectively – and then flick your hand and fingers forward. This gives the illusion that you've actually thrown the card.

Step 4
From the front, if the card is palmed correctly, it's impossible to see anything behind the magician's hand. You can even work this into a sequence of real card throws at speed.

Trick
Do It Yourself NO. 1

Difficulty: 1

Objective

To get a member of the audience to choose a card in secret – then you tell them what it is.

How To Do It

This is a trick that relies on math but doesn't involve any complicated counting or deck setup. It's very simple and as long as you remember the one simple rule, you can't go wrong.

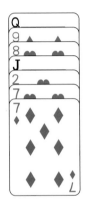
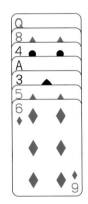

Step 1

Give the deck to a member of the audience and tell them to shuffle it, cut it and generally do what they like with it. Then, deal out three cards face up in a row. After that, deal another card on the first, then one on the second, then another on the third. Make sure the cards are staggered so everyone can see what they are. Continue like this until you've laid 21 cards in three rows of seven, as shown above.

Step 2

Get someone in the audience to pick a card and then remember it. Then, get them to tell you which column the card is in. Pick up one of the columns next to it, then pick up the chosen column and then the other one. Deal the cards again as you did in Step 1. Get them to tell you which column the card is in now, and then pick up the columns in the same sequence as before – another column, the chosen column, and the

third column. Deal and then repeat one more time. In total, you will have dealt, chosen and then collected the cards three times.

Step 3

Give the deck to a spectator. Tell them you're going to spell the magic word ABRACADABRA (make sure that you can!) and that they should lay one card face down for each letter of the word. On the last 'A' tell them to deal the card face up. It's always their chosen card.

Tricks
Nine Is a Magic Number

Difficulty: 2

Objective

To guess the non-face card that's been picked out by the audience without looking at it.

How To Do It

This trick uses simple math and a bit of counting. If the audience member follows your instructions to the letter then it will always work, no matter what card they choose.

Step 1

Give someone the deck of cards and then turn your back. Tell them to shuffle the deck and then select a non-face card, show it round, and place it face up on the table. Think for a second and then say it's too hard to guess. Get them to deal out the same number of cards as the

card they chose – very quietly – face down in a pile next to it (if they chose the 9 of spades they deal nine cards, if they chose the 6 of hearts, then six cards and so on).

Step 2

Claim that it's still too hard. Get them to do the same on the other side of their chosen card. Whereupon you think for a little longer, apologise, and say it's still too hard.

Step 3

Now get them to turn their card over and then deal nine cards on top of it. If they ask why nine? Tell them nine is a magic number.

Step 4

Have them discard the rest of the pack and pick up the cards from the table and shuffle them thoroughly. Turn round and take the cards from them. Fan through and discreetly count them. Then comes the math: take away ten and divide by two. That gives you the number of the card they chose. For example, if there are 22 cards, then $22 - 10 = 12$ and then $12 \div 2 = 6$. If there's only one card of that face value in your hand, you can also tell them the suit.

Trick
Double-Deck Prediction

Difficulty: 3

Objective

To predict the card that a member of the audience will pick without seeing it.

How To Do It

This requires two identical decks and a minimal setup. Because of it's simplicity its a trick favored by street magicians, who like an easy setup, and by beginners, who like anything that's easy! With some good patter, it works well and will convince a willing audience.

Step 1

Take two identical decks, then put the same card on the top of each. In our example, we're going to use the ace of hearts.

Step 2

Give one deck to a member of the audience and tell them they mustn't look at any of the cards because that deck contains your prediction. That's the card that you think you can get someone else to choose.

Step 3

Now give the other deck to another member of the audience. Without looking at the cards, have them fan through and choose a card at random. It's

important that they do not look at this card.

Step 4

Tell them to put it on the top of their deck and then hand that deck to you. Now, you want to do a double lift – picking up the top two cards. In that way, you pick up the card they actually chose and your planted card underneath it.

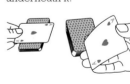

Step 5

Show it to the audience. Then get the person holding the other deck to turn over their top card. It will also be the ace of hearts.

Trick
Simple Card Bend

Difficulty: 1

Objective
To tell the audience the name and suit of a card without appearing to look at it.

How To Do It
Like many other of the techniques included in this book, this works much better if you can work in some patter to distract your audience. If they don't see what you're doing they'll be unable to guess the secret of your success. Although this can be used on its own as a simple trick, it's also a useful technique that you can use elsewhere.

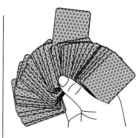

Step 1
Shuffle the deck using your preferred method, then fan out the cards face down. Make a big show of not caring which card the spectator chooses (in fact, you don't care because it doesn't matter) and then tell them to remove it from the pack.

Step 2
Get them to give you the card with the back facing toward you. Hold it as shown with your thumb on the bottom and your two fingers on the top.

Step 3
As soon as you take the card, bend it between your thumb and finger until you can see the pips at the bottom left hand corner. We've exaggerated here just to show you the hand position. Now you know the card, start the chat, stroke the back of the card with your other hand, look the spectator in the eye while you ask them if they're happy with their choice of card... then reveal the name and suit of the card.

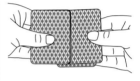
Trick
About Face

Difficulty: 5

Objective
To count out four cards in front of the audience and have one of them turn over of its own accord.

How To Do It
This trick uses only four cards; you need to be able to move two of them together, as if they were one. This is the only hard part of the trick and you'll be able to master it with only a little practice. The great thing about this is that when you're good, you can do it right under someone's nose and they'll never suspect a thing.

Step 1
Arrange four cards of the same kind like this, with three face down and one face up. The other three

cards are also kings – you'll just have to take our word for it.

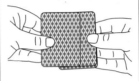

Step 2
Square the cards up and then, holding them as above, use your left thumb to take the top card across. Say: 'One'.

Step 3
This is the tricky part. Slip the card in your left hand between your first and second fingers. Then, use your right thumb to slide the next two cards over as if they were a single card. Say: 'Two'.

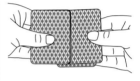

Step 4
Reach underneath with your right hand and take the card you passed over in Step 2. It should now be underneath the last card in your right hand – you've got two cards in each hand. Now, you can pass the top card in your right hand across and say: 'Three', and then pass the final card and say: 'Four'.

Step 5
Fan the cards out slowly counting: 'One, two, three, four.' The fourth card is, impossibly, face up.

Trick
Sort Yourselves Out

Difficulty: **2**

Objective
To get an audience member to arrange the pack, cut it nine times and then deal into 13 piles of four of a kind.

How To Do It
This trick only requires that you set the deck up to run in suits, ace low to king high, and that the audience member follows your instructions exactly. After you've prepped the deck you don't need to touch the cards again.

Step 1
Prepare the deck in suits from ace low to king high, as shown in the illustration. Then, put one suit on top of the other to form the prepared deck of cards.

Step 2
Get someone to count 21 cards from the top. They must not deal them, but count them, so they stay in the same order – we've turned them over so you can see. If they deal the cards as normal, this order will be reversed and the trick won't work!

Step 3
Tell them to put the cards they've just counted off under the rest of the pack. Then get them to do a full cut of the deck, not once

or twice, but nine times. They can cut the cards anywhere they like so long each one is a full cut.

Step 4
Now tell them to deal out the top 13 cards into two rows. Then deal a second card on top of each of the 13. Then deal a third card. Then deal a fourth card so you end up 13 piles of four cards, face down.

Step 5
Tell them to turn the piles over at random. They'll discover that each pile is made up of the same four cards. Fantastic!

Trick
Black and Red Decks

Difficulty: 2

Objective

To convince a member of the audience that they'll be able to split the deck into a pile of red cards and a pile of black cards without looking at them, even when dealing them in any order.

How To Do It

This is a great trick that uses an ordinary deck of cards and requires only the simplest of setups. You start it off and then get a member of the audience to finish laying down the cards. It requires no sleight of hand at all, only a simple twist of one hand at a vital moment at the end of the trick.

Step 1

Set the deck up as shown in Prepping a Deck NO.2 on page 147. So, from top to bottom the pack goes two red, one black, one red, two black, one red,

22 red and 23 black, making a total of 52 cards.

Step 2

Hold the deck in one hand face down. Tell the audience that it's easy to pick out red and black cards if you let your instincts take over. Demonstrate by calling out the first seven cards, pausing and speeding up, as if being prompted by your muse. Just before you lay each card, say out loud whether it's black or red. Lay them in two piles. Since you know the order of the first seven cards, you can say: 'Red, red, black, red, black, black, red.' Then stop.

Step 3

Tell the audience it's their turn. Take a red card from the little face-up pile and put it in front of them, and then take a black card and do the same. Tell them you want them to start dealing cards, face down onto the two piles – red on red and black on black.

Step 4

Of course they won't understand. Tell them to do as you did and use their intuition, but to lay the cards face down on top of the red and black face-up cards. Tell them it doesn't matter what order they lay the cards. Follow their instincts. As they start to lay, all you need to do is count the cards. When they've laid the 22nd card, tell them to stop. Card 22 is the last red card in the fixed deck; all the rest of the cards will be black.

Step 5

Tell them it's too easy and you're going to change things around. Take a black card from the little face-up pile in front of you and put it on the pile of red cards in front of them, face up. Then take a red card from the little pile and put that face up on their black pile.

Step 6

Tell them to lay down the rest of the cards, but this time follow the new markers and lay black cards on the black pile and red cards on the red pile. You don't have to count the cards.

Step 7

Pick up the pile that started red and turned black. Because of the way the deck is arranged, the cards laid by the audience member will be all red and then all black. Fan them out face down with just the two markers showing.

Step 8

Divide the fan at the black marker card, put it down and then turn the cards on top of it over. They're all black. Do the same with the red cards. Easy.

Step 9

Pick up the other pile and fan it out as before. This time, because of the way the deck's arranged, the cards will be in the opposite place to where you want them – all the red cards on the black marker and all the black cards on the red marker. Here's where the sleight of hand comes in. Fan the deck face down and

Trick
Black and Red Decks (continued)

this time, pull out the two marker cards and put them down.

Step 10
Then, with the fan still in your hand, turn it over and lay its cards facing up. This will reverse the position of the red and black cards and make it seem as though they were laid in the correct order.

Black and Red Decks: A Variation
If you'd prefer more control over the trick, then you can try this simple variation. Some magicians prefer it and argue that it's more faithful to the original trick, which was invented by an amateur magician called Paul Curry and was said to be a favourite of the Great British wartime prime minister, Winston Churchill.

Instead of letting a member of the audience deal the cards, you keep control of them at all times until the end of the trick. So, deal the first pre-ordered set of seven cards and then put out a red marker and a black marker and start laying the cards down on each. (Some people find this easier than trying to count the 22 cards when they're being laid by someone else; remember that an unskilled member of the audience may lay two cards at once, or change their minds and try and move cards between piles.) After the 22nd card has gone down, switch the markers and continue until all the cards have been laid down.

Ask a member of the audience to pick up the pile that starts red and turns black. While they're doing that, you gather up the second pile. Get them to lay theirs down however they like, while you can do yours correctly: put down the two mark cards and then turn the fan over with a flourish to lay them down reversed and therefore in the correct order.

Trick
Simple Prediction

Difficulty: **6**

Objective
To predict which card a spectator will pick at random from the deck.

How To Do It
This trick uses a simple riffle force to move the card on the bottom of the deck to any point in the pack that a spectator cares to choose. What's nice about it is that you write down the name of the card on a piece of paper first, so it looks as though you've predicted the card they pick.

Step 1
Before the audience arrives, pick a card, make sure it's on the bottom of the deck and then put the deck face down. Then, write the name and suit of the card on a piece of paper, fold it into a square

and give it to the spectator to put in their pocket. Tell them you're going to make them choose that card from the pack. Don't let them look at the paper.

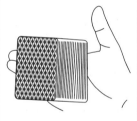

Step 2
Fan the deck out as above so it has a smooth edge.

Step 3
Transfer the cards to your other hand and offer them to the audience. As you do, use the fingers of your first hand to carefully slide the bottom card away

from them. Here we've turned the pack over so you can see.

Step 4
Riffle through the deck with your finger and ask them to say when to stop.

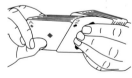

Step 5
Shown from underneath, you can see that we're really going to force the bottom card into the break, making it look like that was the card they'd chosen. Turn the top part of the deck over and get them to inspect the piece of paper in their pocket.

Trick
Do It Yourself NO.2

Difficulty: 2

Objective

To have a member of the audience pick a card, lose it in the deck and then find it again themselves.

How To Do It

This is a great little trick that needs no preparation, no sleight of hand and almost no counting. You never even need to touch the cards, making it a real brain teaser for anyone watching.

Step 1

Pass the deck to a member of the audience and get them to examine, shuffle and cut it. Turn your back. Ask them to think of a number from one to ten and then deal out two piles of cards of that same number – so if they think of a six, the piles have six cards each.

Step 2

Get them to turn one of the piles over and show everyone the card on the bottom. Tell them to remember that card.

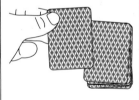

Step 3

Put the pile with their card on top of the deck. Next, turn over the top card and say whether it's red or black, then put it face down on the table. Look at the next card and do the same. It doesn't matter what colour the card is because all you're doing is counting to 11. When the eleventh card has gone down, say: 'Stop'.

Step 4

Tell them to pick up that pile and put it on the deck. Then, they take the second pile, which they made in Step 1, tell you how many face cards it has – this is just a diversion – and put those cards on top of the existing pile.

Step 5

As they lay each card face down, get them to spell out HERE IS MY CARD. Turn over the last one and it's the card they chose.

Trick
Reverse Card Trick

Difficulty: 4

Objective
To have a member of the audience pick any card and return it to the pack. Then you find it.

How To Do It
A simple trick with a little bit of preparation and not much sleight of hand. You'll need to misdirect the audience at one point, but that involves a nice, natural movement that's easy to do.

Step 1
Take an ordinary 52-card deck and turn the bottom card so it's facing up. Then put the empty card packet in front of you on the table. That's it. You're now ready to do the trick.

Step 2
Fan the cards out face down taking care not to reveal the bottom card, which is face up. Ask a member of the audience to pick a card and look at it.

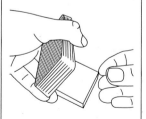

Step 3
While they're doing that, square up the cards in from the fan, making sure your left hand hides the top of the deck so you can flip your hand palm up so that the single reversed

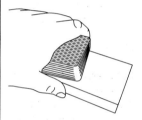

card is now on top of the deck. Get them to slot their card into the pack.

Step 4
While talking to them, reach over with the hand holding the cards and move the empty packet to one side. As you do, turn the deck again.

Step 5
The deck's now the right way up. So just fan the deck to find their card, but be careful not to expose the card at the bottom.

Trick

Court Fours

Difficulty: 2

Objective

To rearrange the court cards without seeming to do anything of the kind.

How To Do It

This is a neat trick that works by itself. Some magicians tell a story to go with it but you can make up any patter you like because you don't really have to think about the trick.

Step 1

Take out all the court cards from the pack and then arrange them as above. There should be an ace, king, queen and jack in each pile. Stagger them so as to make sure the audience can see all the cards.

Step 3

Now you can cut the cards once, wave your hands over the deck and even say the magic word if you like at this point.

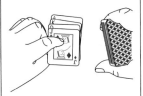

Step 2

Gather the cards up one pile at a time and put one on top of the other. This naturally rearranges them into the order we want.

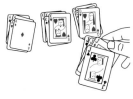

Step 4

Then deal the cards one at a time to make four piles. Turn the piles over and the cards have magically rearranged themselves into their correct families.

Trick
Riffle Find

Difficulty: 4

Objective
To find a card in a shuffled deck without seeing it.

How To Do It
This is a minor classic that's almost impossible to detect as you allow anyone in the audience to riffle shuffle the cards and cut the deck. It's a nice simple setup too.

Step 1
Remove one entire suit from the deck and put it in order from ace low to king high. Then pop it on top of the deck. We've chosen spades and turned the cards over so you can see.

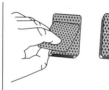

Step 2
Cut two thirds off the deck, put it down, and then put the remaining cards on top of that to complete the cut. Then, get a spectator to cut the deck – say, roughly in half – and remove a card. This will certainly be a card from your sequence.

Step 3
Turn your back. Get them to show the card around and then replace it anywhere in the pack. In this example it's the 8 of spades.

Step 4
Get them to do a riffle shuffle and then a full cut, then another riffle shuffle, and a second cut. If they can't riffle, do it for them.

Step 5
Turn the deck over and go through the cards. Despite the shuffles and cuts placing cards between them, the original suit still runs in order, except for one card. In our case, the 8 of spades.

Trick
Spell Your Card

Difficulty: 4

Objective

To have a spectator choose a card from the deck, replace it and then find it in the deck by 'spelling' it out.

How To Do It

This trick is fun to do because it never fails to put a smile on the audience's face. You'll need to know the Si Stebbins setup from page 146, and along the way we'll also do the easiest of false shuffles. Just make sure you can spell.

Step 1

With the deck in Si Stebbins setup, fan the cards and have the spectator choose one at random. Get them to look at it and remember it.

Step 2

While they're doing that, we do the first part of the trick – guessing their card. Sneak a glance at the card above it in the deck. In this example, it's a 3 of spades. Thanks to Si Stebbins, you know the next card in the sequence – the one they chose – is the 6 of diamonds. Put the packet in your right hand to the bottom of the deck.

Step 3

Casually count in the number of cards it'll take to spell out the name of their card – and then get them to put it back into the deck there.

Step 4

Do the Not-So-Fancy False Cut on page 129 and then deal the cards face down, spelling out the name of their card as you go. Then, turn over the next card. It'll be the one they chose.

Trick
Simple Separation

Difficulty: 4

Objective

To let someone have a packet of red and black cards and mess them up. Then you re-sort them into a black pile and a red pile without looking at them.

How To Do It

This is a great, quick little trick that requires no skill, no sleights and no counting. You need to pull out 12 cards from the deck, but you show them to the audience.

Step 1

Take out any six black cards and any six red ones – it doesn't matter which. Put them in order red, black, red, black and so on, as shown here.

Step 2

Give the packet to a spectator and turn your back. Tell them to turn the top two cards over so that they're now facing up, and then cut the deck. Tell them they can do this as many times as they like.

Step 3

Still with your back to the audience, get them to place the deck in your hands. Then turn round so that the cards are behind your back and they can't see what you're doing.

Step 4

Pass the top card into your other hand. Then turn the next card over and put that on top of the first card. Continue with this sequence, until the cards are all in your other hand.

Step 5

Square the deck and deal the cards into two piles. You've magically separated the cards into a red face-up and a black face-down pile, without looking at them.

Trick
Snap Card Change NO.1

Difficulty: 6

Objective
To change one card into another right in front of the audience.

How To Do It
There are several variations of the Snap Card Change trick, but this is probably the easiest because it relies only partly on sleight of hand – the other key component is a little bit of misdirection, when you make sure the audience is distracted by something else so they're not looking where the action is.

Step 1
Hold the pack face up with your first finger at the front, the other three resting lightly along the side and your thumb on the edge of the front left corner. The secret to setting this trick up correctly

is what's called a double lift – where you pull two cards from the deck while making it look as if there's only one. Choose any cards you like, just make sure they're quite different, preferably a face card of red or black suit and a plain card of the other.

Step 2
Lift the top two cards fractionally using the corner nearest to your little finger and then rest them on it. The lift should be slight enough so that even someone sitting close by can't tell. This makes it easier to pick up the top two cards while pretending to just pick up the top card.

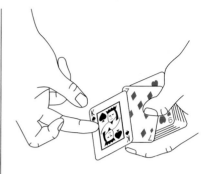

Step 3

Pick the top two cards up from the deck using your thumb and middle finger as shown here, being careful to make sure the audience can't tell you actually have two cards in your hand instead of one.

Step 4

Place the card (actually two cards) on top of the remaining deck like so. It should cover about half of the top card, thus making it easy to hold it securely in place, but also easier to make the switch.

Step 5

Here's where it gets interesting. Use your thumb to pull the top card back into line with the rest of the pack to expose the card underneath. As you do, flick the revealed card down onto the table and then flip the entire deck toward you to conceal the card that was originally on top. The real skill is the smooth movement of this final flourish and reveal – getting the timing right between pulling back the top card, flicking the card underneath it to the table, and then twisting the pack back toward you so no one can see the top card takes practice.

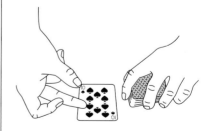

Step 6

And here's the card that was originally underneath the top card now revealed on the table and the hand turned over (and the real top card safely out of the way).

Trick
We Three Kings

Difficulty: 2

Objective
To get an audience member to separate the kings through the deck and then watch as you magically bring three of them together.

How To Do It
This neat trick needs minimal preparation and little sleight of hand – you can introduce a break into the deck if you want to, but it's not necessary. If you can make up a little story, that'll help.

Step 1
Separate the four kings from the deck beforehand. Place one of them on the top. You're now ready to start the trick.

Step 2
Give the remaining three kings to an audience member. Tell them that they like to travel together and when separated, will find each other. Get the audience member to put one king on the top of the pack, one on the bottom and the other anywhere in the middle. Here we've turned the deck so you can see.

Step 3
Let them cut the deck in half so the bottom half becomes the top half.

This puts the two kings that were on top into the middle, with the king that was on the bottom on top of them. This produces a run of three kings. Deal the cards face up and make up a story of how the three kings travelled through the pack until they found each other.

Step 4
Depending on where they cut the deck, the other king may turn up first. You can cover this in the story – 'oh, there's, always one who gets there early' – or make sure you hold the pack when they put the cards back and keep a finger break so you can cut the deck under the middle king so it is on the bottom. We've exaggerated the break so you can see the king.

Trick
Matchmaking

Difficulty: 2

Objective
To make seven pairs of red and black cards, no matter which ones the spectator chooses.

How To Do It
This trick is simple to set up and easy to perform. Yet the results are quite baffling because there's no apparent way to fix the spectator's choice of cards. In fact, it's all to do with the setup.

Step 1
Take out seven red cards and seven black cards. Put the rest of the pack to one side.

Step 2
Ask a spectator to shuffle the deck. Take it back, fan it, and say that you'll need to make a few tweaks before you can start the trick. Sort them into blocks of red and black.

Step 3
Turn the cards face down. Say you're going to deal seven cards each, but that the spectator can choose whether to accept a card. If they say 'yes', deal the card face down. If they say 'no' you get the card.

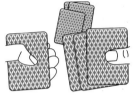

Step 4
When you deal their cards, place one on top of the other. When you deal yours, take your cards placing each underneath the previous one.

Step 5
When you both have seven, ask them to lay their first card face up, then lay your first card; in each case your card will be the opposite colour to their card.

Trick
I Know Where You're Going

Difficulty: 1

Objective
Here's a lovely, simple 'mind reading' trick that allows you to tell the audience member which card they're going to pick.

Step 1
Arrange red and black cards in the pattern shown here. It doesn't matter which cards you choose or whether the reds and blacks are diamonds or hearts or if the blacks are spades or clubs; the important thing is that the colours are arranged just so.

Step 2
Tell the audience that you're going to let them pick any black card, but that with a few simple instructions you'll get them to end up at the card of your choosing – the black card in the middle of the bottom row. Tell them it doesn't matter what card they choose, that you know where they're going to end up.

Step 3
Let them pick any black card. Next, tell them to move up or down to the next red card, then left or right to the next black one, then diagonally to the next red card, and then up or down to the next black card.

Step 4
No matter which black card they choose to start with, they will always end up on the central black card on the bottom row. They can't help it!

Trick
Vocally Challenged

Difficulty: 4

Objective
Someone goes through the pack saying each card out loud. You tell their chosen card by listening to the tone of their voice.

How To Do It
This is another trick that relies on setting up the deck correctly beforehand. After that it only requires concentration on the part of the magician while you 'listen' to the spectator's tone of voice.

Step 1
Prep the deck as follows: Take out one card of each suit. Then, pick a suit and put six cards from it on top and the other six cards on the bottom of the deck. We're choosing hearts.

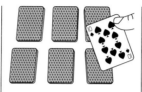

Step 2
Give the cards to a spectator and have them deal out six face down – the top six hearts in our case. Then, add cards to each pile one at a time until all the cards are gone. This will put your chosen suit on the top and bottom of each pile. Have them pick a card from any of the piles, look at it, remember it and put it on top of any of the piles.

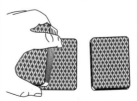

Step 3
Tell them to gather up the cards into individual piles, then put the piles on

each other to complete the deck.

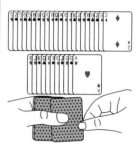

Step 4
Have them deal out the deck a card at a time face up, saying the name of the card as they lay it down. Say you're listening to their voice, that a change in their tone will give the game away. In fact, the arrangement of the cards means that apart from the first and last hearts, in our case, all the others should be in pairs – except for the one that's separated by their chosen card. In our case, the 10 of spades.

Trick
One, Two, Three, Four

Difficulty: 2

Objective

To get a spectator to pick any card from a row of eight and then successfully guess the card without looking at it.

How To Do It

This only needs the barest of preparation and no skill at all. It is, however, an intriguing little trick that works every time and will genuinely baffle the audience.

Step 1

Prepare the deck before the audience arrives. Find all the 4s and then put them on the top of the deck. Then find all the 3s and put them on the top of the deck. Now you're ready to begin.

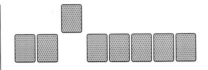

Step 2

Deal out the first eight cards in a row like this. Then, get a member of the audience to pick one of the cards without looking at it by sliding it away from the others toward them. Because you know the order of the cards, you'll know whether they picked a 3 or a 4.

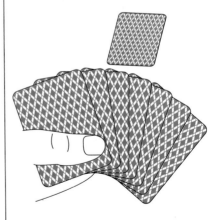

Step 3

Gather up the remaining seven cards, starting from the left and putting each subsequent card under the other – thus

preserving the sequence, which now runs three 3s followed by four 4s. Pop these on the top of the deck.

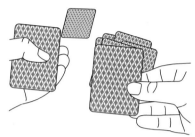

Step 4

Start dealing from the top of the deck. When you've dealt off seven cards, tell the audience that they can tell you when to stop dealing cards whenever they like; because of the way the deck is set up it doesn't matter how many cards you deal after the first seven.

Step 5

Once they've said 'stop', put the remaining cards to one side and then square off the cards you've just dealt. Now, you need to remember what card it is that the audience member picked back in Step 2. If they picked a 3, you

need to deal out three cards in a row. If they picked a 4, go to Step 7.

Step 6

Deal the remaining cards in your hand onto the row of three, one at a time, so that there are three piles of two cards, then three piles of three and so on, until there are no cards left. Turn over the first card. It's a 3. So are the other two. Turn to the audience and say 'your card is the last 3'. Which it is.

Step 7

If they chose a four, deal out four cards in a row, then add a second card to each pile, then a third and so on until you have no cards left. Turn over the first card. It's a 3. Turn over the other cards in sequence. They're all 3s. Say to the audience: 'Four 3s? That's too much of a coincidence. That tells me your card is a 4.' Which it is.

Trick
Eights Are Up

Difficulty: 3

Objective
To make the 8 of hearts 'rise' through the pack from where a spectator has placed it.

How To Do It
This trick needs only a very simple setup and uses a break or finger lift at the very beginning. It's also a good trick for novices because you can make the break before the trick commences.

Step 1
Take a normal deck and remove the 8 and 9 of hearts. Put the 8 face down on the top and then put the 9 on top of the 8.

Step 2
Use your little finger to make a break underneath the 8. This will make it easier to take the top two cards as if they were one.

Step 3
Lift off the top two cards as if they were one and show them to the audience. Say 'I might have known it. The 8 of hearts always has ideas above its station. Let's see if we can't put it in its place.'

Step 4
Put both cards face down on the deck. Then really lift off just the top card, the 9, and, keeping it face down, put it in the middle of the pack. Let it stick out a tiny bit and then flash it to the audience. The top of the '9' will cause the audience to assume it's the top of the '8'.

Step 5
Square the deck and put it on the table. Get someone to turn over the top card. It'll be the 8 of hearts.

Trick
Card 27, Where Are You?

Difficulty: 2

Objective
To present the audience with a seemingly random deck, have them cut it as many times as they like and still be able to find a specific card.

How To Do It
To set this up you'll need to refer to page 146, which explains how to create a Si Stebbins sequenced pack that an audience won't spot and that can survive multiple complete cuts.

Step 1
Prepare the deck in the Si Stebbins sequence. Tell the audience that you've got a particular card on your mind and you're determined to find it.

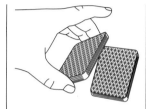

Step 2
Get them to give the deck a complete cut. Then ask them if they'd like to do it again. And again. The beauty of the Stebbins sequence is that it remains intact no matter how many full cuts the audience make; and because they cut the deck themselves, they're unlikely to suspect.

Step 3
When they've finished, explain that you're just going to square the deck up and as you do, casually sneak a look at the bottom card. In this example it's the 2 of spades.

Step 4
Remember that Stebbins sequences the pack in a continuous circle, each following on from the other in the same way. So, knowing the bottom card allows us to work out what the top card is – we just add three and go to the next card in the suit sequence, which is diamonds. Knowing that the top card is the 5 of diamonds also allows us to know that the 27th will be the other red five – because of the sequence it has to be. Tell the audience you're going to find the 5 of hearts, deal 26 cards face down and then turn the 27th one over. Amazing!

Trick
Faster, Faster

Difficulty: 4

Objective
To have an audience member pick a card at random from the pack and then help you find it, even if they don't want to.

How To Do It
There's no preparation required, but you need to be confident about forcing a card from the top to the bottom of the deck.

Step 1
Shuffle the deck and then fan the cards in front of the audience. Ask if there's anyone out there who's excitable and get them to choose a card and look at it. Be sure to tell them that you must not see it.

Step 2
Tell them to put the card back on top of the deck. Make no attempt to look at it. Now you want to force the card to the bottom of the deck, using a false shuffle from earlier.

Step 3
With the card on the bottom, use a standard Hindu Shuffle. About halfway through, take the packet with the chosen card on the bottom and use it to square up the deck by tapping at the end. It looks odd here, but it's actually a natural movement that allows you to see the card they've chosen. Finish the shuffle.

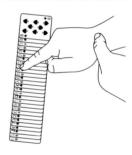

Step 4
Now you know what the card is, you can offer to let anyone in the audience shuffle or cut the deck before fanning it on the table. Guide the person's finger along the deck, feeling for their pulse in their wrist. When they approach their card, claim their pulse is racing, they're getting excited and so on, before revealing the card.

Trick
Court Pairs

Difficulty: **2**

Objective
To show all of the court cards and then rearrange them without appearing to touch them.

How To Do It
This is an elegant and simple trick that demonstrates how to produce a seemingly complex illusion by changing the position of a single card. This particular trick uses all of the face or court cards.

Step 1
Before the audience arrives, take a deck of cards and put the queen of diamonds on top of it (we've turned it over here just to show you). When the audience is there, take out all the other court cards and lay them in a

mess on the table. It's unlikely anyone will spot the missing red queen.

Step 2
Pick the cards up and order them: red queen, two black kings, two red jacks, two black queens, two red kings, two black jacks.

Step 3
Tell the audience you're going to show them the six pairs of court cards. Then, take two off the top (red queen and black king) and put them on the bottom of the packet.

Step 4
Show the next pair and do the same. Keep going until you've actually shown the queen of hearts (which is the only red queen you have) twice. No one will notice. The queen of hearts is now on the bottom of the pack.

Step 5
Pop the cards you're holding on top of the original deck (where you placed the other red queen in Step 1). Now deal the cards out in twos and they've been rearranged magically into matching pairs.

Trick
World's Greatest Card Trick

Difficulty: 4

Objective

To have a spectator choose a card at random and then find it. Then choose another card at random and miraculously transform that card into the first one.

How To Do It

This trick gained brief notoriety as 'the world's greatest card trick', and while it's nothing of the sort, it is effective and baffling. Best of all, it employs only a small deceit and a minor setup.

Step 1

You'll need a complete deck of cards plus one duplicate from another deck with a different colour or design on the back. Pick something reasonably memorable, perhaps a face card. We're using the queen of hearts.

Step 2

Put the queen of hearts from the original deck on the bottom of the pack and then put the duplicate from the other deck under that. You now have 53 cards with two queens of hearts on the bottom.

Step 3

Spread the cards out as if you were doing a Basic Ribbon Spread (see page 143) taking great care not to reveal the back of the bottom card. Cover it by saying something like 'I'm still working on my ribbon spread' and laughing. Then, have an audience member take a card out of the pack at random, look at it and then remember it.

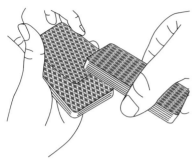

Step 4

Gather the cards up, being careful not to expose the different-coloured one. Do a slow Hindu Shuffle (see page 92) and get the audience member to say 'stop' before you finish. Then get them to pop their card on top of the cards held in your left hand.

Step 5

Put the rest of the cards in your right hand on top of the pack in your left. This produces the correct card order for the trick. Their card – which you still don't know – followed by the duplicate queen of hearts with the different back followed

by the 'real' queen of hearts. We've turned the cards over here so you can see.

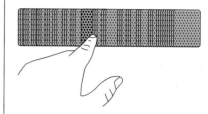

Step 6

Do a ribbon spread. As you do, say that you're looking for something in the deck that will reveal their chosen card. When the different-coloured card appears, you can point to that.

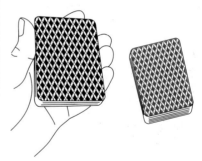

Step 7

Set the cards before the different-coloured card to one side. Then pick up the other packet and square it off.

Trick
World's Greatest Card Trick (continued)

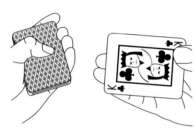

Step 8
Then do a double lift, picking up the different card and the card underneath it, which is the one selected by the audience in Step 3. Show it around.

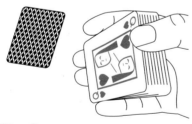

Step 9
While the audience is distracted, put both cards face down on the deck and take off the top card only, saying: 'So let's put your card down here.' In our example, they think it's the king of clubs, while we know it's the duplicate queen of hearts. Then, take the packet you've been working with and put it on top of the other packet. This will ensure the

original queen is on the bottom of the deck. We've turned it over so you can see.

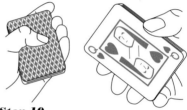

Step 10
Do another Hindu Shuffle and get the audience to tell you when to stop. Then show them the bottom card in your right hand. This will be the queen of hearts.

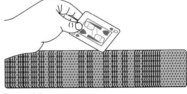

Step 11
Do a Hindu Shuffle to 'lose' the queen of hearts in the pack. Then, spread the cards again. Say you're hoping the queen will reveal herself like the last card did, maybe in the same way, maybe she'll wear different colours. When you can't find her say something like: 'Well, I don't suppose…' then turn over the different coloured card laid down in Step 9. This will be the card they chose in Step 10.

Trick
Divined Card

Difficulty: 4

Objective
To 'divine' the card that a member of the audience will pick before they know what it is themselves.

How To Do It
This is a genuinely baffling trick that only requires a normal deck, a bit of simple counting and a pen and paper. In fact, the audience do most of the work.

Step 1
You need to know what the 34th card in the deck is before you start. In our example it's the king of hearts. Write down the name of a card on a piece of paper, fold it and give it to a spectator. Tell them you're going to find this card.

Step 2
Cut the deck, but be careful not to cut more than half. Give the top half to a spectator, have them shuffle it and spread it on the table. Then remove three cards at random from the spread and turn them over.

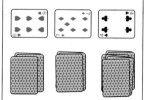

Step 3
Pick up the rest of the spread and put it on top of the deck. Look at the three cards. In front of them, lay as many cards as needed to bring the total to ten; so if it's a 4 of clubs, lay six cards. Court cards all count as ten and you don't lay anything, aces count as one.

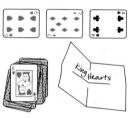

Step 4
Get someone to add the three cards together. Lay that number of cards face down. Turn over the next card and get the spectator to open the piece of paper in their pocket. It'll be the same card.

Trick
Snap Card Change NO.2

Difficulty: 8

Objective

To change a single card into another right in front of the audience by clicking your fingers.

How To Do It

This is the more difficult version of the original trick on page 188. It requires less setup, no props, but real dexterity and practice to make it work properly. Once mastered, it's even more impressive than the other snap because of the speed at which it's performed and the complete lack of an obvious explanation.

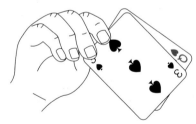

Step 1

Start by taking two cards from the deck and then lining them up so that it only looks as though you've got one card. You can do this before actually starting the trick or – if there's an audience present – by using the double lift technique described on page 188 in the previous Snap Card Change trick. Choose any cards you like, just make sure they're

obviously different – preferably a face card of red or black suit and a plain card of the other.

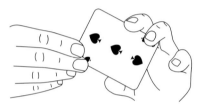

Step 2

Okay, here's how you want to be holding the cards (or as far as the audience is concerned, card). Use your first and second finger on the corner like this. Hold it at slight angle as well, with the pack angled down a little bit as shown.

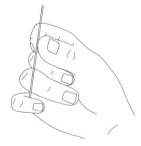

Step 3

Meanwhile, use your thumb round the back of the cards to grip it. It's important to hold the cards just so in order to be able to achieve an effective 'snap', a bit like clicking your fingers. With practice this is the fastest way to switch the cards – and thus the most deceitful.

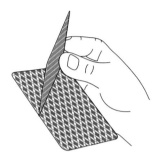

Step 4

This is the key movement. Slide the back card up with your thumb, guiding it with your first finger, while at the same time keeping hold of the front card with your second finger and the joint of your thumb. If you find it hard at first, try just gently snapping your thumb and second finger and you'll soon get the hang of it. If you have problems with the move then you're probably holding the cards too tightly.

Step 5

With the snap complete, it looks as though the card has simply changed. Only a really observant member of the audience will notice that instead of two fingers at the front of the card, you're now holding it with one.

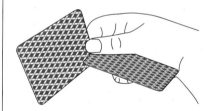

Step 6

That's because round the back of the card your second finger is busy keeping the original front card hidden horizontally behind the other card.

Trick
Three Jacks

Difficulty: 4

Objective

To repeatedly deal three jacks to a
spectator, despite appearing to order the
cards so as to make it impossible – then
to top that by dealing them four aces.

How To Do It

The pack needs some simple
preparation and there's a small sleight of
hand involved. This is made easier if you
can sit in a chair with arms.

Step 1

Prepare the pack as follows. Find the
four jacks and put them on top of the
deck with the jack of spades at the top,
followed by the diamond, the club, then
any old card (we're using a 2), followed
by the last jack. Take the four aces,
alternate them with any old card and
then add a couple of cards underneath.
Then, take this ace sequence and turn it
upside down and put it on the bottom of
the deck.

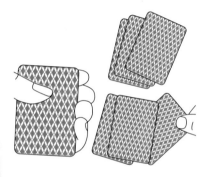

Step 2

Tell a spectator you're going to show
them a move that card sharps use. Deal
the top card to them, a card for yourself,
then the third for them, the fourth for you,
the fifth for them and the last one for you.
Make sure you slip your last card under
the other two.

Step 3

Say 'I know my hand's rubbish', pick it up
and put it on top of the deck. Get them to

turn their cards over. They'll have three jacks. Pick them up and then drop them back on the table so that when you pick them up, they'll be ordered like so: black jack, red jack, black jack.

Step 4
Put them on top of the deck. Deal again in exactly the same way. Put your cards on the top of the deck again. Get them to turn theirs over. It's those jacks again! They won't realize that this time it's actually the other red jack.

Step 5
Gather and order the jacks the same as Step 3 and put them on top. Deal the cards again. This time you can deal them straight because it doesn't matter. They'll get two black jacks and one red one.

Step 6
Pick up both hands and then put them on top of the deck. Then make a little fuss over bringing your chair closer to the table. When the hand with the deck is out of sight, flip the deck over.

Step 7
This time say you're going to try harder and give them four jacks. Deal them one, then one for you, then one for them and so on until you've both got four cards. Get them to turn their cards over. They have four aces.

Turning the Deck
This is one of the few tricks we've included that includes a set of cards prepared and placed upside down on the bottom of the deck. Practise turning the deck upside down so the audience doesn't spot your move.

Trick
Shake Change

Difficulty: 4

Objective
To change one card into another right under the audience's noses.

How To Do It
A subtle variation on the various snap change tricks explored elsewhere, the shake change is more delicate and when combined with flourishes even harder to spot. As before, pick two cards that are visually very different like the king of hearts and the ace of clubs to heighten the effect.

Step 1
Take your cards and place them back to back. Here we're showing them in a mirror just so you can see what's going on.

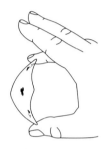

Step 2
Grip the cards with your thumb and third finger at opposite corners as shown here. Then get some extra leverage by bending the cards as much as you think you can get away with.

Step 3
What you want to do is reach over the top of the card with your first finger and then pull it back toward you so it pivots on the 'hinge' made by your thumb and third finger.

Step 4
When the cards have swapped over, whip your first finger out from behind it and then you're ready to change it back. This trick is easy to do in slow motion, but the magic comes from introducing the shake of the hand while you're pivoting the card. This is what makes the audience believe that you've somehow managed to actually change the card.

Trick
Retrieving Ace

Difficulty: 3

Objective
To show the audience four aces, then have them pick a card at random and watch as you use one of the aces to find their card.

How To Do It
This is a great little trick with a simple setup and an easy technique: the finger lift. Even beginners can work it very well, as the lift can easily be concealed by the card in your other hand.

Step 1
Take a 52-card deck and make a show of pulling out the aces and displaying them fanned out next to the face-up deck as shown.

Step 2
As you square the aces up, ready to put into the pack, you want to do a little finger lift so that the card underneath – in this case the 7 of hearts – is raised from the pack.

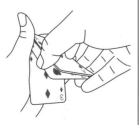

Step 3
Square the aces up, pop them on the bottom of the deck, and then with your right hand take all four aces and the 7 of hearts underneath them.

Step 4
Turn the deck over and put the packet on top. Say: 'All four aces are on top.' Deal them face down – you've actually dealt three aces and a 7. Fan the deck and get someone to choose a card, look at it and then put it back on top of the deck – on top of missing ace.

Step 5
Cut the deck. Turn over the four cards. Where's the missing ace? Turn the rest of the pack over one by one. The missing ace has 'found' their chosen card.

Trick
Top and Bottom

Difficulty: 2

Objective
To have a spectator choose a card seemingly at random and then find it for them without knowing what it is.

How To Do It
Again, this is another great counting trick that doesn't really require any counting – which makes it our favourite kind. Use a normal deck and let an audience member do most of the work!

Step 1
Hand the deck over to a member of the audience and then turn your back. Get them to shuffle and cut the deck as much as they like; it really doesn't matter what they do. Then tell them to deal anywhere between ten and 20 cards, very quietly onto the table in two equal piles.

Step 2
Tell them to put any remaining cards away. Then to choose one of the piles and look at the top card. This is their card and they need to remember it.

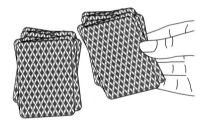

Step 3
Ask them to take a few cards from the top of the other pile and put them on top of the pile with the card they've just chosen. Tell them to hide the other pile so you can't guess how many cards are in it – not that it matters.

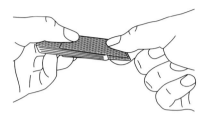

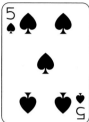

Step 4

Tell them to put their chosen card back. Turn round and ask for the pile they're holding in their hand, the one that has their card in it. Take a card from the bottom and a card from the top as shown here.

Step 5

Put the two cards down on the table in front of you. Then, continue pulling cards from the pile in your hand in exactly the same way. If there's an odd number, that card just goes on the top of the pile.

Step 6

Take the bottom card from your pile and turn it over on the table. Tell them that's not their chosen card. Then turn over the top card and say the same.

Step 7

Pick up both cards and put them on the top of your pile. Then get the audience member to pick up the pile they hid in Step 3. Tell them to deal their first card, face down on the table. Match it with one of your own. Get them to lay their next card and you do the same. Carry on until they lay their last card. When they do, turn over your next card. It'll be the one that they chose in Step 2.

Trick
Twenty-Six

Difficulty: 4

Objective

To have someone cut the deck into three, shuffle the cards, pick one at random and then return it to the pack, only to have the magician find it again.

How To Do It

This uses a very simple setup that only requires you to know what the 26th card in the deck is. After that, the trick works itself with only one small, easy bit of counting.

Step 1

Make sure you know what the 26th card in the deck is. In this example it's the king of hearts.

Step 2

Put the deck on the table. Get a spectator to cut two thirds off the top and put it next to the original pile. Then, cut half off the top of the second pile and put that next to it. You've now got three relatively even piles.

Step 3

Have them shuffle the last packet and then look at the top card and remember it.

Step 4

Get them to shuffle the first packet and then drop it on the last packet. Then pick both up and drop them on the middle packet.

Step 5

Turn the cards over. Starting with the one you placed, count left. The 26th card will be the one they chose. If you count past the end of the deck, continue from the start.

Trick
The Clock

Difficulty: 3

Objective
To tell a spectator the hour of the day they've chosen and then to show it matches the card prediction you've already written on a piece of paper.

How To Do It
This trick is a real winner because there are two points when the audience will be amazed: first when you tell them the hour they've chosen, then when you demonstrate your all-knowing powers by predicting the card that sits at that position in the clock face.

Step 1
The trick is played out with the deck face up.

Prepare it by placing any card of your choice as the 13th card in from the face side of the deck – we're using the 8 of hearts. Next, write the name and suit of that card on a piece of paper, fold it up and put it to one side.

Step 2
Give a spectator the deck and turn your back. Have them pick any hour of the day between one and 12. Then they should – very quietly – deal off the same number of cards and put them to one side.

Step 3
Take the deck back and count out the top 12 cards onto the table.

Step 4
Lay the cards out in a clock face starting at 12 o'clock. Find the card you placed in Step 1. Its position tells you the hour they chose. Then, starting at one o'clock, count round to the chosen card, say its name, then take out the piece of paper – it'll match the card.

Trick
Cards From Nowhere

Difficulty: 7

Objective
To make a succession of cards appear
out of thin air.

How To Do It
This sleight of hand is beautifully simple
and effective. There's no arduous
preparation involved and once perfected
it'll leave most audiences open-mouthed.
It suits magicians who enjoy engaging
directly with the audience and is highly
theatrical. It takes a lot of practice though,
hence the relatively high difficulty rating.
Let's make some cards appear.

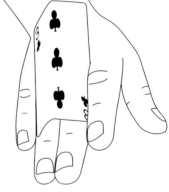

Step 1
Start this trick with just two or three cards
– the exact cards don't matter, but since
you're going to damage them it might
be good if they come from an old pack.
As you get better you can increase the
number to half a dozen, but for now, start
small. Fold the cards lengthways down
the middle so they form an arch, like the
roof of a little house.

Step 2
Next, you want to use your stronger hand
to hold the cards – but behind it, so the
audience can't see. Slot the folded cards
over the backs of your second and third
finger and then hold them in place using
your first and little finger. Next, slide the
cards away from the tips of your fingers
so that the corners are roughly lined up
with your first finger joint and the other
corners are resting on the back of your
hand. By now, you should be able to see
where this is heading.

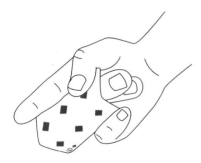

Step 3

You may still have to do some fiddling to position the cards properly. What's important is that you can hold the cards firmly in position without having so much of the two corners exposed that the audience can see them. When you hold your hand out like this, the cards should be invisible.

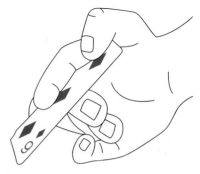

Step 5

This shows the first stage of the snap – we've pulled the top card off the others and it's now held between our first and second finger.

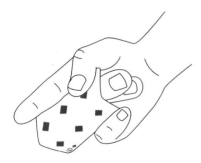

Step 4

To bring the first card into view you need to bend your two middle fingers forward slightly and lift your first finger away so that you can then use your thumb to pull the top card over the second finger and have it snap into view. Here we've turned the hand in the illustration so you can see the movement more clearly.

Step 6

And here's the card pulled fully into view. Notice that the other card is still held firmly round the back of the card. Once you've mastered the technique it's easy to conceal the mechanics by making a movement with your hand such as hitting a drum or snapping your fingers to conceal what's going on even more effectively.

Trick
Swap

Difficulty: 3

Objective
To give a member of the audience two cards and then swap them round before their eyes.

How To Do It
In order to do this trick you'll need a second deck with the same backs. If you've got an old set with a few cards missing, that'll do fine. You'll also need to be able to do a double lift.

Step 1
You need two cards that are the same with another card in the middle – make sure they're noticeably different. Show the cards to the audience so they can see the order and put the rest of the pack to one side.

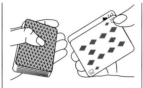

Step 2
Put the three prepared cards on the deck. Next, tell the audience you're going to show them the top card. Do a double lift to take the top two cards and show them around as if they were a single card. We've deliberately shown both cards here for the illustration.

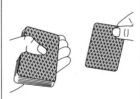

Step 3
Pop both cards back on the deck. Then take and lay down the real first card on the table and say: 'right, that's the 10 of diamonds' or whatever it

is. In fact, it's the real top card, the 3 of clubs.

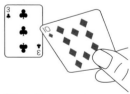

Step 4
Then, do a second double lift, picking up the top two cards as one and show the audience. Again, we're showing you both.

Step 5
Put them back on the pack and take the real top card. The audience thinks the face-down card is the 10 of diamonds (it's the 3 of clubs) and think that in your hand is the 3 of clubs (it's the 10 of diamonds).

Trick
Odds and Evens

Difficulty: 2

Objective
To move a card between piles without touching it.

How To Do It
There's no preparation or sleight required, but it looks like there must be.

Step 1
Ask someone to place both hands on a table, fingers bent under. Take two cards from the top of the deck, say: 'two cards, even' and put them between their first and second fingers.

Step 2
Put two more cards between the other fingers

of one hand, each time saying 'two cards, even'. After that, put a single card between the first finger and thumb.

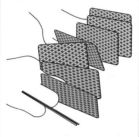

Step 3
Put two cards between the fingers of the other hand and two cards between the first finger and thumb. Each time say 'two cards, even'.

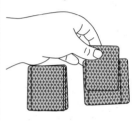

Step 4
Next, take a card from one hand and a card from the other and say 'two cards,

even'. Put these cards down side by side.

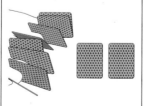

Step 5
Continue taking cards, one from each hand saying 'two cards, even' until your helper is just holding the single card between first finger and thumb. Say that you have two piles, both even and that adding this last card will make one of them odd. Have the spectator choose which pile. Put the card on that pile. Say the magic word, whatever you like, make a few hand movements and the card will magically jump across making the other pile an odd number. (In fact, both piles have seven cards, and adding the last card makes that pile even).

Trick
Order, Order

Difficulty: 2

Objective
To keep a suit of cards running in sequence, no matter how many times you lay two cards at once.

How To Do It
This is a pretty short trick, but it's a cracking one that will bamboozle the audience. You can prepare it in front of them and run through it as many times as you like – it can't be messed up.

Step 1
Pull out one suit and put them in order as shown here – ace high down to 2 low.

Step 2
Tell the spectator you're going to deal the cards face down and get them to say 'double' when they want you to deal two cards at a time, instead of just one.

Step 3
When they say 'double', take one card off the top of the deck and take a second card on top of the first card as shown here. Then lay it down. By doubling this way, you don't actually alter the order of the cards at all.

Step 4
They can get you to double as many times as they like. When all the cards have been dealt, offer to do the whole thing again. Then, when they're satisfied, deal the cards face up to show that the cards are still in exactly the same order.

Trick
Six of the Best

Difficulty: 2

Objective
To pick six cards at random from the pack and guess what they are without looking at them.

How To Do It
This is a great little trick that relies on a single mis-call at the start for its effect. It's very easy to set up (it only requires you to remember the position and name of a single card) and because it's got some audience participation, they'll find it difficult to work out how you're fooling them.

Step 1
Before starting the trick, memorize a card like the ace of hearts and then place it at a specific

location in the pack. In this example it's the ninth card – we've turned it over so you can see.

Step 2
Get the audience some paper and a pen. Tell them you're going to pull six named cards from the pack without looking at them first, and as you pull them from the pack, you'll want someone to write them down. Then, say you're going to find the ace of hearts. Go through the pack, pick a card at random, look at it and say 'Yes, that's the ace of hearts!' no matter what card it is.

Ace hearts
Two clubs
Four clubs
Nine hearts
Eight diamonds

Step 3
Ours is the 2 of clubs, so we place it face down on the table, and remember it. Then we say we're going to find the 2 of clubs and no matter what card we actually pick, we say 'That's it alright!' and add it to the pile on the table. Then we use the card we really picked to predict the next one and so on. When you come to pick the sixth card, say it's the ace of hearts – the card we originally placed – remember where it is and pick it out from the deck. Pick up the six face-down cards and get the audience to read out what's on the piece of paper. As they read out each card, turn it over.

Glossary

Ante The stake in a betting game, especially Poker.

Bid Where you tell the other players in the game how many tricks or points you intend to win.

Blind One or more cards that are usually laid face down away from play and may or may not be used later on, depending on the game.

Book A closed meld or sequence that no other player can add to; often placed face down away from play.

Contract Where you commit to winning a specific minimum number of points or tricks. Contracts are enforceable.

Cutthroat Sometimes used to describe games where there are no partnerships and everyone plays solo.

Deal Where one person doles out a specific number of cards to everyone in the game; usually clockwise, starting from the person on their left.

Declaration What you say when you make a contract to win tricks or points.

Deuce A 2 of any suit, occasionally called a two-spot.

Draw When you take a card or cards, usually from the pack.

Draw trumps Where you try to empty your opponent's hand of trumps by leading with a high trump.

Eldest The first player to receive their cards; usually the player to the dealer's left.

Face card A king, queen or jack; some people also count the ace as a face card.

Face value The number on a card, this is not always what it's actually worth within a particular game when a different value may be assigned.

Flush When you have a group or run of cards all of the same suit.

Follow suit Where you have to follow the previous player's card with one of the same suit.

Foundation Used in solitaire games; the card that you use as the base on which to build a sequence or suit.

Game Usually a specific number of points that, when reached, signifies the end. Games are made up of hands which in are made up of tricks.

Going out When you get rid of your last card, often to win the game, either by playing it to win a trick, using it to complete a meld, or discarding at the end of your turn.

Hand Cards dealt out to each player; there'll usually be a number of hands during the course of a game.

Lay off When you add one or more of your cards to a meld laid on the table by an opponent; for example, in rummy.

Lead When you lay down the first card in a new trick.

Maker Usually the person who calls trumps, but can also refer to anyone who takes on a contract.

Marriage A specific meld made of a king and queen, usually of the same suit

Match Where you duplicate what's gone before either by laying the same cards or making the same bid, bet or contract.

Meld Usually three or more cards that are either the same (like three 7s) or run in sequence (like jack, queen, king), melds are used to score points in a game; sometimes called a combination.

No-trump Used in some trick-taking games where there are no trumps.

Packet Any number of cards, usually more than ten, which may be manipulated as a group in a shuffle, a cut or a flourish.

Pass When you decline to take your turn; whether to play, bid or whatever.

Pip The markings on the face of a card; a 5 has five pips, a 9 has nine and so on.

Plain card Any card that isn't a jack, queen or king; *see also* face card.

Sequence A meld of two or more consecutive cards.

Set A meld of three or more cards of the same kind.

Stock Refers to the cards left after a deal that may or may not be used later on.

Trey A three of anything; occasionally called a three-spot.

Trick A round in a hand, usually, but not always, comprising one turn per player.

Trump The suit that is designated as being higher than the other three suits in a particular trick, hand or game; also refers to the act of laying a trump card on top of a non-trump to win the trick.

Upcard After the hand has been dealt, many games then take a card from the remaining pile and turn it over to form a discard pile; this is the upcard.

Void When you have no cards of a particular suit in your hand.

Wild card A card that can be used in place of any other card; the use and any restrictions surrounding wild cards should be agreed before the game.

Resources

There's a huge variety of Internet pages and websites that are dedicated to playing cards in general, the games, skills and tricks in these pages, and many more besides. Obviously we can only scratch the surface, but here are a few of the more useful ones.

American Contract Bridge League

This site aims 'to promote the fun and challenge of bridge and support educational and playing opportunities for Bridge enthusiasts throughout North America.'
www.acbl.org

BBC

The British Broadcasting Corporation site has a small selection of card games, well explained, including some that aren't in this book such as Mao, Top Trumps, Skat, Kalabriasz and more.
www.bbc.co.uk/dna/h2g2/C906

Bicycle Cards

The virtual home to the classic make of playing cards, favoured by players and magicians the world over.
www.bicyclecards.com

Cards Chat

A lively and informative forum for poker players from around the world. It's a great source of help, tips and advice.
www.cardschat.com

The Card Games Site

Hundreds of games are explained here in a mammoth list organized into alphabetical order and regularly updated.
www.pagat.com

Card Throwing

Actually as the URL suggests, this is actually part of a larger knife-throwing site, but it's got lots of good information about how to throw cards – like whether the Herrmann method is better than the Thurston method.
www.knifethrowing.info/throwing_cards.html#cardtypes

David Blaine

Although he's now more famous for his Houdini-style feats of escape and endurance, Blaine did a great job of making close card magic trendy. Check out the videos on this site, the skill involved is exceptional!
http://davidblaine.flux.com

Design Your Own

Here's an interesting tutorial for computer types, which shows how you can go about creating your own unique playing card design using Adobe Photoshop.
www.webdesign.org/web/photoshop/drawing-techniques/playing-cards.16586.html

Easy Magic Tricks

A good selection of card, close and street magic on video. Some people find watching a moving image easier to understand than following paper instructions. If that sounds like you, then this site is well worth a visit.
www.howtodotricks.com

eHow

Literally hundreds of 'how to' pages relating to the world of card games including how to build a house of cards, how to beat the dealer at blackjack, how to cheat at Spades, how to beat Freecell and many more.
www.ehow.com/articles_2419-card-games.html

Ellusionist

A good selection of very high-class tricks to buy; includes all the equipment and instructions to perform convincing magic tricks close up in a range of different situations.
www.ellusionist.com

English Bridge Union

Beginners and experts will find a warm welcome here; the site is approachable, informative, well laid out and contains an enormous amount of Bridge-related information.
www.ebu.co.uk

Flash Games

A nice selection of free solitaire games that you can play online. You'll need to have the latest version of Flash installed, but your browser will prompt you if you need to do anything.
www.flashgames247.com

Hoyle

There are loads of software card games here, over 150 from the sedate Cribbage to the raucous pleasures of Texas Hold 'em Poker. The site has a free 60-minute trial.
www.hoylegaming.com

International Card Playing Society

Here you will find almost everything that you ever wanted to know about playing cards, all gathered together into a single website. There's also a really neat and helpful world history of playing cards included.
www.i-p-c-s.org

Lady Cadogan's Illustrated Games of Solitaire or Patience

Part of Project Gutenberg – the online archive where books are made available to view or download for free in electronic form – this minor classic is definitely worth a look if you're interested in the different games of patience that you can play.
www.gutenberg.org/etext/21642

Magic Tricks

There are plenty of card-related magic tricks available to buy from this site, including trick decks, packet tricks and instructional DVDs to buy at this site.
http://magicshop.magictricks.com

Masters Games

If you're thinking about playing Cribbage and you want to buy a quality board with some character, then this is a good place to start.
www.mastersgames.com/cat/pub/cribbage.htm

Resources (continued)

Medieval and Renaissance Games

There are plenty of rules for old, less common card games to be found here; and its generally a terrific resource for old-time games of all descriptions. http://jducoeur.org/game-hist/game-rules.html

Playing Card Picture Gallery

A fascinating resource that has pictures of hundreds of different card types, with interesting accompanying text that throws even more light on the subject. www.geocities.com/a_pollett/cardpgal.htm

TM Cards

A source of various card decks to buy online; reasonably priced too. www.tmcards.com

Video Jug

More than just a site for Internet videos, Video Jug specializes in videos that teach visitors how to do stuff – in our case, card tricks. It offers a good selection and is well presented. www.videojug.com/tag/card-tricks

World Bridge Federation

Bags of information here for anyone interested in the world of competitive Bridge – lively and opinionated. www.worldbridge.org

YouTube

The now ubiquitous video-sharing website contains plenty of useful videos showing how to perform a wide variety of tricks and skills. www.youtube.org